S0-ADJ-298

ARTS & CRAFTS
FURNITURE PROJECTS

GREGORY PAOLINI

The Taunton Press

Text © 2015 Greg Paolini
Photographs © 2015 by The Taunton Press, Inc.
Illustrations © 2015 by The Taunton Press, Inc.
All rights reserved.

The Taunton Press, Inc.,
63 South Main Street, PO Box 5506, Newtown, CT 06470-5506
e-mail: tp@taunton.com

Editor: David Heim
Copy Editor: Seth Reichgott
Jacket/Cover design: Rosalind Loeb Wanke
Interior design: Tinsley Morrison
Layout: Laura Lind Design
Illustrator: David Heim
Photographer: All photos by Gregory Paolini, except p. iv, p. 3 (top and bottom), and p. 4 (top) by Randy O'Rourke, p. 4 (bottom) by Barbara Bourne, p. 6 by Anissa Kapsales/*Fine Woodworking* magazine, and pp. 122–141 by Matt Kenney/*Fine Woodworking* magazine

The following names/manufacturers appearing in *Arts & Crafts Furniture Projects* are trademarks: Festool®, Lee Valley®, Masonite®, Plexiglas®, SawStop®, Titebond®, Woodpeckers®, X-ACTO®.

Library of Congress Cataloging-in-Publication Data
Paolini, Gregory.
  Arts & crafts furniture projects / Gregory Paolini.
    pages cm
  ISBN 978-1-60085-781-2
  1. Furniture making. I. Title. II. Title: Arts and crafts furniture projects.
  TT194.P364 2015
  684.1—dc23
                    2014046454

Printed in the United States of America
10 9 8 7 6 5 4 3 2 1

ABOUT YOUR SAFETY

Working wood is inherently dangerous. Using hand or power tools improperly or ignoring safety practices can lead to permanent injury or even death. Don't try to perform operations you learn about here (or elsewhere) unless you're certain they are safe for you. If something about an operation doesn't feel right, don't do it. Look for another way. We want you to enjoy the craft, so please keep safety foremost in your mind whenever you're in the shop.

Dedication

To Frank, Mom, and Mona

Acknowledgments

This is the third book I've written, so you might think it would have been easier to complete than the first two. But somehow it was more of a challenge than the first two combined! Fortunately, I had a great, patient team to help get me through it.

First and foremost, I need to thank David Heim. Technically, David was my editor, but in truth he should be listed as one of the authors of this book; without him, you certainly wouldn't be reading this right now. Thank you, David!

I also want to thank Peter Chapman for his patience and faith in this project. Yes, Peter, I can't believe it's finally done either.

Special thanks to Matt Kenney at *Fine Woodworking* magazine for helping with the chapter on building the sideboard.

There's a handful of folks at the Taunton Press who work behind the scenes that I'd like to thank as well. I've never met most of these people—or I've had only quick email or phone conversations with them—but I know that they worked extremely hard to convert my scribbled manuscript, mediocre photos, and chicken scratch into incredible books. In short, these folks compile great books, and make me look good, too. I really appreciate it!

I'd like to extend thanks to a few folks at my favorite tool companies, too: Michael Williams at Festool®, Rich Hummel at Woodpeckers® Tools, and Matt Howard at SawStop®. Thanks for making some "kick butt" tools that help us woodworkers do what we love to do! But, more important, thanks for believing in me and the team at GPD, and for being companions on this journey.

Speaking of GPD (Gregory Paolini Design LLC, where I teach woodworking and build furniture, millwork, and cabinetry), I definitely need to thank my work family: Shane Hall, Mike Pentland, Phil Carter, Eric Kimes, and David Greenbaum. Thank you so much for helping me through this book.

And thanks, of course, to my family at home: Mom, Frank, Jaime (Jamie), Dave, Jen, Dan, Sheri, and Charlotte!

Last, but certainly not least, I want to thank my wife, Mona. For quite a while she may have forgotten what her husband looked like while he was off building furniture, cabinetry, and a business. Mona, thank you!

Contents

1

A FEW WORDS OF INTRODUCTION

This book celebrates the beauty of wood and the furniture makers who helped launch a new aesthetic movement in the late 19th and early 20th centuries. The movement became known as Arts & Crafts, and the woods those early makers used to great advantage were oak, cherry, mahogany, and maple.

The Arts & Crafts Movement

The style of Arts & Crafts objects reflects a philosophy that arose in England in the mid-1800s. At that time, the Industrial Revolution was running at full throttle, but churning out shoddy goods produced in dehumanizing factories. The critic John Ruskin and the designer William Morris, generally acknowledged as the founders of the Arts & Crafts movement, strived to change that. They embraced the skill of craftsmen and wished to elevate workmen to the status of artists. Medieval architecture and art became their ideal, and they promoted the aesthetic and practical value of plain, well-crafted furniture and other household objects. As Morris put it, the movement intended to make

things "for the people and by the people, and a source of pleasure to the maker and the user." Ruskin's writings and Morris's businesses promoted this philosophy, trying to produce things that everyone could afford.

The English Arts & Crafts movement never achieved its goal of producing fine work for a mass market. But the Arts & Crafts philosophy quickly spread worldwide. In the U.S., many potters, furniture makers, weavers, and architects adopted the Arts & Crafts philosophy. Just as Morris spearheaded the movement in England, Gustav Stickley was the chief proponent of Arts & Crafts in the U.S. He and his brothers established a number of businesses that succeeded in providing durable Arts & Crafts furniture to a wide audience. Stickley also published an influential magazine, *The Craftsman,* which helped spread and popularize the Arts & Crafts philosophy.

The major American Arts & Crafts furniture makers embodied that philosophy with very different designs. Stickley's work, for example, generally features large, square legs, thick stretchers and slats, with exposed tenons and other joinery, as shown in the photos on the facing page. The go-to wood was quartersawn white oak.

OUT IN THE OPEN. One feature that distinguishes Arts & Crafts furniture from other styles is the use of exposed joinery. Shelves in the bookcase above have long through-tenons that are held in place with wedges. On the settle at right, tenons on the rails protrude through the corner posts.

ARTS & CRAFTS, OLD AND NEW

Gustav Stickley, Harvey Ellis, the Greene brothers, and other craftsmen and designers established Arts & Crafts in this country more than a century ago. Today, their work is still valuable and has inspired new generations of cabinetmakers. The style has long been a mainstay in the pages of *Fine Woodworking* magazine. Its second issue included the article on Stickley at top on the facing page. Harvey Ellis was featured in issue #45, shown below the Stickley pages.

SYMBOLIZING A STYLE. The Morris chair is probably the most iconic piece of Arts & Crafts furniture, and it has taken many forms over the years. The Roycroft chair shown here has carved legs.

WEST COAST VARIATIONS. In California, the Greene brothers created a distinctive style featuring exposed pegs and splines, prominent box joints, and furniture with softly rounded edges. Contemporary craftsman Darrell Peart perpetuates the Greene & Greene style, making pieces like this sideboard.

Gustav Stickley

The rebel craftsman of his time

by Carol L. Bohdan and Todd M. Volpe

One of the last great designer-craftsmen to come out of the 19th century was Gustav Stickley. Today, this cabinetmaker and entrepreneur is almost forgotten. But for 15 brief years before World War I, Stickley's 'Craftsman' furniture and furnishings enjoyed great popularity. A change in popular taste and the onslaught of mass-produced goods spelled the end of his success. Now, however, Stickley's work is being rediscovered in attics, barns and secondhand thrift shops and appearing on the more prestigious (and expensive) antiques circuit.

Born in 1857 in Wisconsin, Stickley was trained by his father as a stonemason, but soon left to learn cabinetmaking from an uncle in Pennsylvania. After working in furniture factories and stores, he formed a distaste for the gaudy pieces generally popular at the time and developed instead an admiration for the simple and sturdy forms of the Shaker furniture he had seen.

Stickley was also influenced by the decorative arts coming out of Chicago in the 1870's, one of the pulse centers of the arts and crafts movement in this country. A trip abroad to see 'art nouveau' and English arts and crafts designs convinced him further to purify furniture forms. He became determined to create a personal, streamlined construction that would eliminate most needless decoration, with each article free from pretense, and in his own words, 'fitted for the place it was to occupy and the work it had to do.' He thus, for the most part, avoided the 'tortured and fantastic lines' based on the organic plant forms of which the art nouveau enthusiasts were so fond, preferring to omit 'intrusive' inlay, artificial 'affectation,' and those forms that evoked the past in a "quaint" or historical way.

In his quest to develop a distinctive style, he took the medieval joiner's compass as his symbol and borrowed the motto 'Als ik Kan' ('As I can,' or, more broadly, 'All I

can') from Jan van Eyck because it was 'brief, modest and not always easy to fulfill.'

In turning to earlier craft traditions, he created a mystique around his furniture that would prove most appealing to a public jaded by ornate forms. There was, however, nothing mystical about Stickley's esthetic goals. Furniture, according to him, was to be made 'first of all for daily use and wear ... comfortable, durable and easy to take care of.' It was Stickley's desire to escape the growing influence of the machine over the manufacture of domestic goods, and to address the needs of his time by directing the public toward 'an art that shall strike its roots deep into the life of the people,' emphasizing the ideals of simple hand-craftsmanship, functionalism, easy care and, above all, comfort.

Stickley preferred to work with oak (although he also used chestnut, ash and elm), explaining: 'When I first began to use the severely plain, structural forms, I chose oak as the

Perhaps best known of Stickley's furniture is the Morris chair named after the British philosopher and spokesman for the arts and crafts movement, William Morris. Plant stand is 26 inches high.

Oak lamp (22 inches high) has pale yellow and green stained-glass shade. Bookcase (56 inches high) bears Stickley's label and signature (above). Stickley-designed writing desk (30 inches high, below) has copper hardware and was made in Grand Rapids. Pieces are from author Volpe's collection.

Stickley's 1901 armchair, left, is straightforward, with practically no decoration. Stiles, rails and stretchers are pinned mortise-and-tenon, the tenons carried through in the larger members. The arms of the chair are little more than stretchers, evidence of Stickley's commitment to expressed structure, sometimes to the detriment of comfort.

Ellis chair, below, designed two years later, is also straightforward. But the scaling down of the members and the elimination of through tenons permits our attention to focus on the chair's form, a cube. Its severity is relieved by the comfortable cushion and the graceful, abstract inlays, set off by a grain-obscuring ebonized finish.

The Ellis sidechair, above, exhibits all the characteristics associated with Ellis' designs— graceful and delicate lines, a curved apron, tapering legs and a high back. Ellis had a superb eye for line, as his inlay shows. The pattern, a favorite, shows Mackintosh's influence. It is probably abstracted from floral or human form, and its termination, a torii, the Japanese gate form, reflects Ellis' love for Japanese art. After Ellis' death Stickley altered the stretchers, removed the top rail and sold this version as a standard item until he declared bankruptcy in 1915. *(continued next page)*

Photos courtesy the Jordan-Volpe Gallery

Stickley introduced this desk, left, in 1901. It is absolutely rectilinear, with prominently expressed structural features. It is framed of massively overscaled members, enclosing panels assembled from chamfered, butt-joined and splined boards. The chamfering is echoed in the small door in the desk's gallery. Like the strap hinges and the chamfering, the decorative elements of the desk are purely structural. Large, double-pinned through tenons pierce the front and back legs, and stand slightly proud of the otherwise flat surfaces. The legs, in addition, rise decoratively above the line of the top rails.

Ellis's desk, above, a 1903 design, is a marked contrast to Stickley's. Ellis has followed Stickley's dictate of simplicity, but has subordinated the structure to a refined, pure form with gently tapering sides and a wide overhanging top. The horizontal lip attached to the fall-front, which breaks up this flat plane and reiterates the shape of the overhanging top, might be said to violate Stickley's proscription against applied ornament. But it functions as a handle as well as decoration.

The fall-front desk, left, shows many of the features that Ellis introduced to Craftsman furniture. The deeply arching underrail gives this wide desk a sense of lightness that contrasts with the conscious sturdiness of Stickley's earlier designs. Gently rounded cutouts repeat this curve at the bottom of the plank sides. Ellis has replaced Stickley's expressed structural decoration with his own stylistic signature: the arching curves, the wide overhanging top, a paneled oak back and the attenuated inlay pattern.

Photos H. Peter Curran, courtesy the Jordan-Volpe Gallery

FEDERAL INLAY.
Many of Harvey Ellis's original pieces featured stylized flowers inlaid in the case. Nancy Hiller, a modern-day interpreter of Arts & Crafts, used a similar motif in the hanging wall cabinet shown above.

Charles and Henry Greene, who defined the Arts & Crafts style in California, produced furnishings and houses heavily influenced by Japanese and Chinese design. Table aprons, chair backs, even house rafters featured a distinctive curved "cloud lift" shape. They mainly used mahogany rather than oak, with exposed splines and pegs made of ebony.

Like the Greene brothers, the seminal architect Frank Lloyd Wright designed complete environments—house, furnishings, and decorations—that embodied many Arts & Crafts attributes. He used oak in his early houses and furniture, and created furniture based on simple geometric shapes. Much of his furniture was better for show than use, though; many of his designs were uncomfortable, impractical, or both.

Other major Arts & Crafts figures include Harvey Ellis and Elbert Hubbard. Ellis was an

architect whose designs influenced Gustav Stickley. Many of Ellis's desks and bookcases have slanted or tapered sides; they also include stylized flowers inlaid in the wood, a feature often associated with the Art Nouveau style. Hubbard, a one-time soap salesman, met William Morris on a trip to England and became devoted to the Arts & Crafts philosophy. He established a very successful craft community known as Roycroft in East Aurora, N.Y. At one point, Hubbard employed some 500 workers.

Arts & Crafts furniture is probably more popular now than it was a century ago. Pieces by Stickley and the other original masters are highly collectible (and very expensive). There are also a number of fine furniture-makers who create modern interpretations of the style. These are just four:

Darrell Peart, a professional based in Washington, is the foremost practitioner of the

Greene & Greene style. Another Washington furniture maker, Tom Stangeland, creates pieces reminiscent of Stickley, Greene & Greene, and others. In San Francisco, Debey Zito and Terry Schmitt collaborate on original Arts & Crafts designs embellished with Schmitt's delicate carvings. Kevin Rodel, working in Maine, makes furniture reminiscent of pieces by Charles Rennie Mackintosh, the Greene brothers, Harvey Ellis, and others.

When you make one of the pieces in this book, you'll be helping to perpetuate a style and philosophy that's close to 150 years old.

Choosing Lumber

Wood is a natural material, which began as a living tree. Because of this, it has properties that are unique to it, unlike manmade materials, such as plastic, aluminum, and steel.

Wood has a grain structure that gives it strength along its length. This is evident in house construction, where walls are made of lots of long, skinny studs. You'll see the same strategy in furniture, too. Table legs are long and skinny. The aprons that connect the legs to form the table's base are long skinny pieces as well, just oriented horizontally.

Wood's weakness is across its width, or in line with the grain. If you have ever cut firewood, you know that one blow from an ax along the grain will split a log. And we've all seen the karate master break board after board with his bare hands. Watch closely, though, and you'll see that the karate chops always hit the board in line with the grain.

Wood's grain isn't always perfectly straight, however. As the tree grows, the trunk bends here and there and the grain follows. When a tree is cut down and sawn into boards, the unstraight grain can cause the wood to distort and change shape, resulting in defects we refer to as twist, warping, and cupping. As the tree grows branches, the grain changes direction as well. In lumber, the transition from trunk to branch produces a knot. For strength and stability, work with the straightest pieces of lumber you can find.

When building furniture, be sure you have wood that is sufficiently dried. Avoid wood from a freshly felled tree, which is still full of sap and water. As the water and sap evaporate, the wood will shrink and possibly warp and split. Most commercially available lumber is dry enough to use without problems. Some small mills still produce air-dried lumber, boards stacked and allowed to dry naturally.

POSITIONS OF STRENGTH. In order to utilize wood's natural strength, the components of a piece of furniture are oriented along their lengths. On the legs of this sideboard, for example, the grain runs vertically. On shelves and stretchers, it runs horizontally.

SMALL DRAWBACK. This board has a slight bow in it. A straighter, flatter board will yield a better finished project. You can sometimes remedy minor defects like this at the jointer.

BIGGER DRAW-BACKS. The small knot on the left of this board may add character to the finished piece. But the large knot could compromise the strength of the board. Avoid using wood with such a major defect.

One of the most important things to remember about wood is that it moves. This is why it's so important to start building with relatively dry wood. The material will constantly expand and contract across its width and thickness as the humidity around it fluctuates. (Wood has minimal shrinkage along its length.)

Some craftsmen describe wood as a sponge—and they're not far off. On a cellular level, wood is just like a sponge. During humid summers, wood absorbs the excess moisture in the air and expands. As winter approaches and the air becomes drier, the wood contracts. If you ignore wood movement, neglect it, or try to restrict it, your furniture will fail. Fortunately, there are strategies for dealing with wood movement.

USE QUARTERSAWN WOOD

There are two main ways to cut a tree into boards. *Flatsawn* means that all the boards have been sawn in the same plane; this yields the greatest number of boards from the tree, but the boards are the most prone to twist and warp. *Quartersawn* boards have been cut at an angle across the log; imagine a log divided into quarters, with boards sawn out of each quadrant at an angle. Quartersawn boards are the more stable; wood movement is typically half that of flatsawn lumber.

Some species of quartersawn lumber—particularly white oak—exhibit beautiful figure that the original Arts & Crafts furniture-makers exploited. The figure, called ray flake, is a pattern of light streaks running diagonally across the face of the board. The streaks are properly known as medullary rays, and they transport nutrients radially in a living tree.

USE THE RIGHT SPECIES

Wood movement varies from one species to another. The woods most often used in furniture-making—oak, cherry, walnut, mahogany, and the like—are favored in part because they are relatively stable.

BUILD IN ROOM FOR EXPANSION

Obviously, a wide board will expand more than a narrow one. That's why a tabletop is attached with fasteners that have some wiggle room, allowing the top to expand and contract freely. You'll see one type of fastener in chapter 7, the Greene & Greene desk: Z-shaped connecters are screwed to the top but fit into slots in the stretchers between the legs, so they can move back and forth. Likewise, the center panel in a door will also expand and contract; to prevent it from buckling, it's usually made smaller than the opening and not glued into place, so it can shrink and swell freely.

The Projects in This Book

Making furniture in the Arts & Crafts genre can be very rewarding for beginning woodworkers as well as seasoned veterans. The simple styles, honest joinery, and straightforward lines are well within the grasp of someone new to the craft. At the other end of the spectrum, complex styles may present a challenge to makers who have spent their entire lives honing their skills.

This book presents various furniture projects in several Arts & Crafts styles. Each project introduces a skill set or technique to be mastered. Each subsequent project builds upon the previous skills while introducing new ones. Each project includes a cutlist—a list of every board in a project, with its dimensions. The cutlists include a measure of board feet to help you plan. It's prudent to double the board-foot figure to give yourself some leeway to match grain and figure, to allow for losses from milling, and to allow for mistakes (not that you will make any!)

As you work through this book, your talents will improve as you create beautiful and functional pieces of furniture for your own home. Here's hoping you find building Arts & Crafts furniture as rewarding as I do.

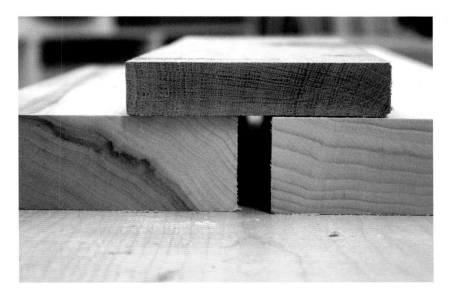

THREE GRAINS. The board at bottom left is riftsawn, which orients its growth rings at 45 degrees to its face. The board at bottom right is flatsawn, meaning that its growth rings are parallel to the face. The board on top is quartersawn, so its growth rings are perpendicular to its face.

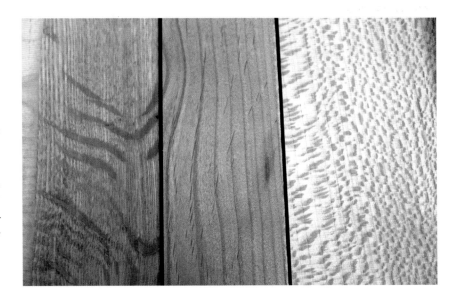

THREE RAYS. Prominent figure like ray flake varies with the wood species. It is very prominent on the quartersawn oak (left) and the quartersawn sycamore (right). The alder board in the center has less conspicuous ray-flake figure.

2 STICKLEY-INSPIRED FRAME

One of the biggest names in the American Arts & Crafts movement is Gustav Stickley, the leading proponent of the philosophy in this country. He was the oldest of five brothers, who all became prominent furniture makers and were sometime business partners and sometime competitors.

We'll begin our journey of building Arts & Crafts furniture with a Stickley-inspired frame for a mirror. It's a simple project that embodies classic Arts & Crafts proportions and construction. It's made from quartersawn white oak, the wood used in much original Arts & Crafts furniture. Although the frame consists of only four pieces, making it introduces you to some essential woodworking skills: milling boards to their final dimensions, marking and hand-cutting a mortise-and-tenon joint, and gluing up the piece neatly and accurately.

Mill the Lumber Flat and Square

I usually label the boards for a project with chalk, then I rough-cut the boards a few inches oversize. That makes them easier to handle and provides a margin for error (mine or Nature's).

STICKLEY-INSPIRED FRAME

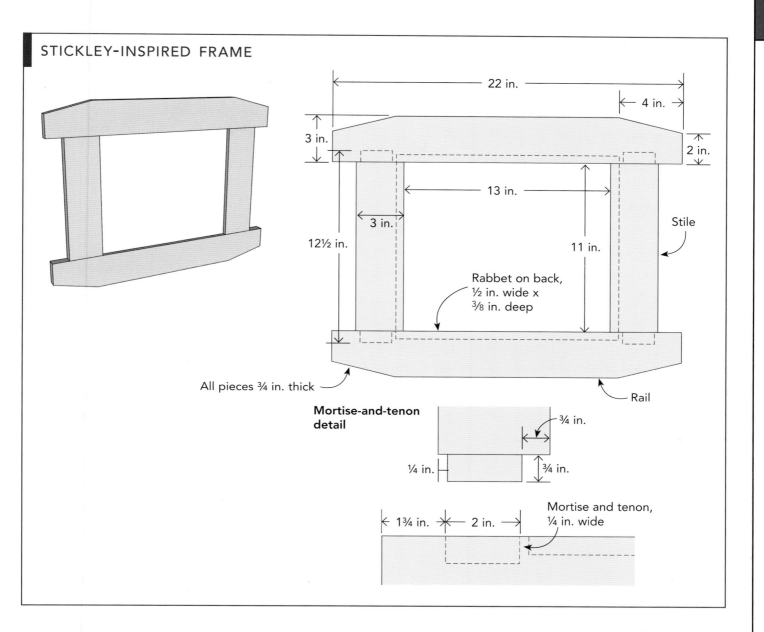

22 in.

4 in.

3 in.

2 in.

13 in.

3 in.

Stile

12½ in.

11 in.

Rabbet on back,
½ in. wide x
⅜ in. deep

All pieces ¾ in. thick

Rail

Mortise-and-tenon detail

¾ in.

¼ in.

¾ in.

1¾ in.

2 in.

Mortise and tenon,
¼ in. wide

MATERIALS

QUANTITY	PART	THICKNESS*	WIDTH*	LENGTH*
2	Rails	¾	3	22
2	Stiles	¾	3	12½

Total board feet: 1½

* Measurements are in inches.

GO FLAT. Begin milling wood for a project by pushing one face of a board across a jointer. That removes minor defects such as twist, warp, or cupping, and makes that side of the board perfectly flat.

GO ON EDGE. The next step is to turn the board to joint one edge. This cleans up rough edges, removes more defects, and yields two adjacent surfaces that are flat and at right angles to each other.

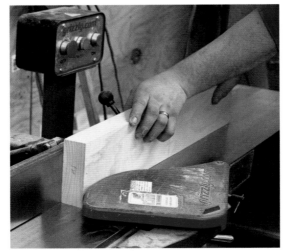

CHECK YOUR PROGRESS. Hold the board up to the light and place a square on the jointed faces. Any light showing between the square and the wood reveals an edge that still needs more work at the jointer.

I store the remainder of the boards for future use. There's no sense in milling an entire board if you don't know how you will use the leftover part in the future.

Before you can begin cutting pieces to size or creating joinery, you must make the lumber flat and square. That's a prerequisite for laying out final dimensions and joints correctly, and most shop machines require flat edges in order to cut and shape the boards safely.

The first step is to flatten the workpieces. You can do that with a long handplane, but the white oak has a tendency to tear out, leaving small voids. The best tool to flatten rough lumber is the jointer. Place the workpiece on the infeed table of the jointer and, with consistent downward pressure, move the piece from right to left over the cutterhead and onto the outfeed table. Use push blocks to keep your hands away from the cutter, and button or roll up shirt sleeves for safety.

Don't be concerned about the position of the jointer fence at this point; it's there only to help you guide the board across the cutters. Run the board over the cutter repeatedly until the face is dead flat.

Next, position the flat face against the jointer's fence and joint one edge of the board to make it flat and square to the jointed face. Use a square to be sure the fence is perpendicular to the table, and adjust it if need be. It's also important to keep the workpiece tight against the fence.

Now you're ready to make the board the proper thickness, something best accomplished with a thickness planer. Place the flat, jointed face of the workpiece against the planer's bed, so the machine can dress the opposite face and make it parallel to the jointed face.

Remove only a small amount of wood with each pass, sneaking up on the final thickness. Plane all the boards of a particular thickness at the same time. "Batch planing" ensures that all the pieces will be uniform in thickness. For this project, the four frame pieces are ¾ in. thick.

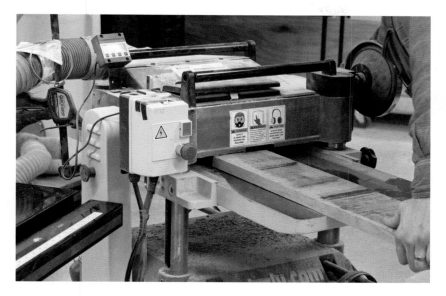

ABOUT FACE. Use a planer to mill the other wide face of a board. This step flattens that face and ensures that the two faces are parallel.

WORK SAFE

Never run a piece of wood less than 12 in. long through a jointer or planer. The piece could get caught in the tool's cutterhead and kick back toward you with enough force to cause serious injury.

Cut the Boards to Size

At this point, your workpieces are surfaced on three sides, or S3S, as they say at the lumberyard. Now, you can cut them to their final width and length.

I begin this stage of the milling by ripping the pieces to width on the tablesaw, which I have outfitted with a ripping blade. My standard operating procedure is to set the rip fence and cut all the pieces of a particular width at the same time. Once I have one batch ripped, I reset the saw fence and cut the next batch of similar-sized boards. In this project, though, all the components are 3 in. wide, so I have only one fence setting. Most projects will have boards of several different widths.

Change the ripping blade for a combination, or crosscutting, blade and cut one end of each

THREE DOWN. This piece of oak has been surfaced on three sides, or is S3S. It's ready to be ripped to its final width and crosscut to length.

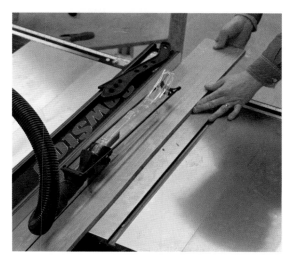

FINAL CUT. For consistency, rip all the boards of a specific width at the same time. I keep a push stick on the rip fence so I can quickly grab it when cutting narrow boards.

WORK SAFE

Tablesaws can be dangerous. Always use proper technique and all necessary safety equipment. Guide narrow stock past the blade with push blocks or push sticks.

CORRECT TECHNIQUE. When crosscutting, hold the workpiece against a fence attached to the tablesaw's miter gauge. Attach a stop block to the fence to cut identical pieces to the same length.

WORK SAFE

Never use a tablesaw fence as a stop when cutting pieces to length with a miter gauge. The offcut could get jammed between the fence and the blade, creating a dangerous kickback situation.

piece to square it up. Use the saw's miter gauge to support the work. Be sure the miter gauge is exactly 90 degrees to the blade; if it isn't, your frame will not be square.

To finish sizing the pieces, measure and mark the finished length on each board. Install a stop block on the miter gauge's fence at that distance from the blade. Be sure the blade cuts on the waste side of the line. For this project, set the stop block at 22 in. from the blade for the rails, 12½ in. for the stiles. The stop block ensures that identical parts will be exactly the same length. Consistency trumps accuracy in this situation.

Cut the Mortise and Tenon Joints

With all the frame parts cut to size, arrange them as if they were already joined together. Put the faces with the best grain and figure up and mark a big X on them in chalk. Those marks will help you keep the pieces oriented properly.

LAYING OUT AND CUTTING THE MORTISES

Using basic layout tools such as a combination square, a try square, and rules, outline the mortises on the inner edges of the rails. Each mortise begins 1¾ in. from the end of the board and is 2 in. long. I draw lines across the edge of the board with a square and a pencil to indicate the ends of the mortises. Then I set a marking gauge or combination square to ¼ in. and draw lines parallel to the board's face to indicate the position of the long mortise walls. Use a marking gauge to lay out the shoulders of the tenons on the stiles, ¾ in. from the ends. You'll mark the thickness of the tenons after the mortises are cut.

Make the mortises first. (It's easier to cut a tenon to fit a mortise than vice versa.) Remove the bulk of the waste at the drill press. Chuck a ¼-in. Forstner bit or brad-point bit into the drill press and set its stop to cut just a touch deeper than ¾ in. Then clamp a fence to the drill press

LAY OUT JOINTS. Use a pencil and square to mark the length and width of the tenons as well as the position and outline of the mortises.

DRILL MORTISES. Begin shaping the mortises by drilling a series of holes to remove most of the waste. Leave a small bit of wood between the first series of holes to keep the bit drilling straight. A second series of holes takes care of the rest of the waste.

CLEAN UP. Use a sharp chisel to square the ends of the mortises and remove the ridges left by the drill bit on the side walls.

table to keep the boards aligned as you drill multiple holes for the mortises. The fence doesn't have to be anything more than a square piece of scrap. It's almost impossible to lay out and drill a hole perfectly centered on a workpiece, so orient each piece with the X on the reference face toward you. Then the distance between the edge of the bore and the fence will always be consistent, your frame will lie flat, and all the joints will be in the same plane.

Rough out the mortises by drilling a series of holes the length of the mortise. Space them more than 1/4 in. apart, so you leave some wood in between. Come back and drill out the

remaining waste. This method helps prevent the bit from drifting, or veering at a slight angle.

With the bulk of the material drilled out, clamp the workpiece onto your bench or in a vise and use a very sharp 1/4-in. chisel to square up the ends. The endgrain of the white oak requires just a little more than hand effort to cut, so I tap the chisel with a small mallet. Use a wider chisel to remove the ridges left by the drill bit to give the mortises flat, smooth walls. Paring this long grain should take no more than hand effort, but you will want to make sure the long mortise walls stay perpendicular to the edge. Clamping a block of wood to the face of

SCRIBE LINES. Use a marking gauge or marking knife to create definitive shoulder lines for the tenons.

REFINE CUTTING LINES. Before sawing the tenons, use a chisel to enlarge the groove left by the marking gauge. This creates a channel for the saw to follow.

the frame member can help guide you and keep the mortise square.

LAYING OUT AND CUTTING THE TENONS

With the mortises cut, set a marking gauge, referenced against a rail face marked with the X, to the same width as the mortise. Use that setting to define the thickness of the tenons. This ensures that the frame members remain in plane, even if the mortises are off center. To begin shaping the tenons, lightly tap a chisel into the marking-gauge lines to deepen them slightly. This will help guide the saw while cutting, for a more precise cut and cleaner shoulders.

To cut the tenons by hand, use a saw with a backed blade—one with a strap of metal wrapped around the edge. Begin by cutting the tenon cheeks. A tenon saw or dovetail saw, designed to rip, is ideal for this task. Clamp the piece in a vise and cut the narrow cheeks first, then the wide cheeks (also known as faces).

With the cheeks cut, finish the tenons by cutting their shoulders, using a backsaw designed

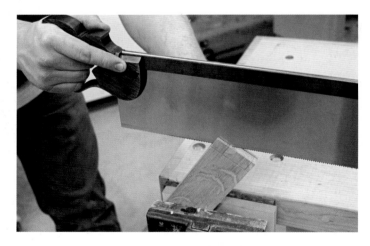

TENON CHEEKS FIRST. Use a tenoning saw, which has teeth ground for ripping, to cut the cheeks of the tenon.

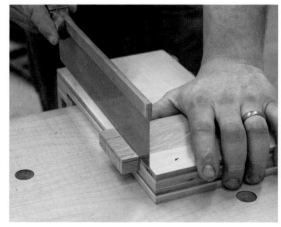

SHOULDERS NEXT. Switch to a saw designed for crosscutting to cut the tenon shoulders. A bench hook (a piece of plywood with cleats on opposite faces) helps steady the piece as you cut.

for crosscutting. Always position the saw so the blade is on the waste side of the line, to avoid cutting away too much wood, or cutting into the portion of the frame that will be exposed. The kerf from the previously cut cheeks provides a stopping point, so you don't accidentally cut into the frame member.

The fit of a mortise-and-tenon joint is critical. If you need a mallet to force the pieces together, it's too tight. If the tenon just slips into its mortise, the joint is too loose. A well-executed mortise-and-tenon joint should go together by hand, but with some effort. Once assembled, the joint should stay together on its own and not come apart when you move the pieces around on the bench. Test-fit each joint, taking one or two passes with a rabbeting block plane to refine the size of the tenon until you have it just right.

Trim the Rails

The final saw cuts to be made create the long bevels on the rails, which give this frame its signature shape. (You can see the bevels in the photo sequence on p. 20.) Lay out the bevels by placing tick marks 4 in. from each end and 1 in. down from the outside edge. Connect the tick marks and saw away the waste with a rip saw. Accuracy isn't critical, because these cuts are decorative, but if you veer too far off the layout lines, the frame will look lopsided. To clean up the saw marks, clamp the two rails side by side in a vise and use a sharp plane to smooth the sawn surface on both pieces at once.

Test the Fit, Glue the Frame

With all the joinery completed, it's time to assemble the frame. But before I commit to gluing any joints, I like to do a dry run. This reveals any problems that could occur during the actual glue-up, such as a joint that doesn't fit quite right or an assembly that isn't square. The dry run lets me rehearse the glue-up process, to be sure I have the right clamps and everything else I'll need at hand.

FINE CUTS. Use a rabbeting block plane (shown) or a shoulder plane to pare the cheeks of the tenons for a perfect fit. Steady the workpiece with a bench hook.

DRY FIT. Assemble the piece without glue to double-check the fit of the joints and to gather everything you'll need for a successful stress-free glue-up.

CLAMP CAREFULLY. Be sure to place the clamps in line and centered on the joints. Otherwise, the clamping pressure can pull the joint out of square or skew it so it won't lie flat.

SPREAD THE GLUE. Apply some glue to each mortise, then use a small brush to evenly coat the walls of the mortise. Also apply a light coat of glue to the tenon cheeks.

The dry run also helps me decide where to position the clamps. A clamp that's not perfectly centered on a joint can actually pull a project out of square or out of flat. With this project, an out-of-flat frame will result in a mirror that is distorted (and reflects like one in a funhouse).

If everything seems fine in the dry run, move on to the glue-up. Regular white or yellow glue will be plenty strong enough for this frame; in fact, the glue joint will be stronger than the wood surrounding it. With most white and yellow glues, you have only about five or six minutes to assemble the frame, from the moment the first drop of glue hits the tenon until you tighten the last clamp. If the glue-up takes more than 6 minutes, the bond will be compromised because the glue has begun to set.

Most people use too much glue on their joinery. Ideally, you want only enough glue to create a bond between the cheeks of the tenons and the walls of the mortises. Any excess will become squeeze-out that will have to be cleaned off lest it interfere with finishing. I apply a small bead of glue on each of the long mortise walls and spread it around with a small brush. Then, one by one, I spread glue on a tenon and insert it into its corresponding mortise.

REMOVE SQUEEZE-OUT. Any glue that squeezes out of the joint must be completely removed. If it isn't, finish won't adhere later. Use a slightly damp cloth to remove the excess.

Place a clamp across each pair of joints and tighten them evenly to pull everything home. Measure the frame's diagonals to check the assembly and ensure that the corners are square. If the diagonal measurements are the same, the frame is square. If they're not, bump the frame on the long corners until the diagonal measurements are identical. Once the clamps are snug, wipe away any excess glue squeeze-out with a barely damp rag. Allow the frame assembly to cure overnight before removing the clamps.

Cut a Rabbet, Add the Mirror

In order to install the mirror into the frame, you'll need to make room for it by cutting a rabbet. Install a ½-in. bearing-guided rabbeting bit into your router and make ⅛-in.-deep passes around the frame's inner perimeter until the rabbet is ⅜ in. deep.

The mortise will have rounded corners, so use a sharp chisel to square them up. Once you've done that, ease the edges of the frame, sand it, and finish it. I used a simple shopmade wipe-on finish, which I call 321, for this mirror. See chapter 11 for more on finishing.

WORK SAFE

When routing the inside of a frame with a handheld router, always move the tool in a clockwise direction to maintain control and avoid a dangerous self-feeding situation.

RABBET FOR THE MIRROR. Use a router fitted with a rabbeting bit (left) to make a rabbet on the back side of the frame. The bit has a bearing that rides along the frame to guide the tool. Move the router clockwise around the opening (below).

CLEAN UP THE CORNERS. Use a sharp chisel to square up the rounded corners left by the router bit.

FITTING THE MIRROR

To turn the frame into a mirror, head to your local glass store with the frame and have them cut a piece of ⅛-in.-thick mirror glass to fit the rabbeted opening. Some glass shops will install the mirror for you, but in case yours doesn't, here's what to do.

Lay the mirror into the rabbet and cut a piece of ⅛-in.-thick plywood backer to help support and protect the mirror. Secure the backer in place with 18-gauge trim nails, putting them a few inches from each end of the rabbet. Drive the nails in just enough to keep them in place. Do not force the nails or backer downward, as this will distort the mirror.

To keep out dust, apply a paper backing to the frame. Begin by applying ½-in.-wide, two-sided tape around the perimeter of the frame's opening. Cut a piece of kraft paper about 1½ in. to 2 in. larger than the opening. When applying the paper, you'll want to avoid creases, so start at one corner, seating the paper against the tape. Work evenly along adjacent edges while you

ADD ADHESIVE. Stick strips of double-sided tape around the edge of the frame to hold the paper that will keep dust from getting inside the frame.

FINAL ASSEMBLY. Slip the mirror glass into the frame first, followed by a thin wood backer board, which you can see at the left.

ADD THE PAPER. Begin at one corner, as shown, and press a piece of kraft paper onto the tape. Don't worry if the paper seems loose.

SECURE EVERYTHING. Carefully drive brads into the frame to hold the mirror and backer in place.

press the paper in place, always keeping the paper taut until you reach the opposite corner. Don't worry about waviness or minor wrinkles in the paper at this point. Remove the excess paper, using a razor knife and a straightedge.

Now spritz the paper with a light mist of water. Don't soak the paper; just make it damp. Use a hair dryer or heat gun to blow-dry the paper. Keep the dryer moving continuously so you don't singe the paper or harm the finish. As the paper dries, it will shrink and become as tight as a drum.

The last step is to install a hanger. I prefer to use screw eyes and picture wire. Measure roughly a third of the way down the frame and install a screw eye on each side. The wire between them should be twisted to anchor it to the screw eyes and should extend up to just above the opening of the frame. This will provide plenty of support. To hold the bottom of the mirror off the wall a bit, I apply small plastic cabinet bumpers to the bottom edge.

The only thing left is to find a place to hang this heirloom piece.

TRIM THE EDGES. Use a sharp razor knife and a straightedge to trim the paper.

HEAT-SHRINK. A blast from a hair dryer or heat gun quickly dries the paper and shrinks it tight.

GIVE IT A SPRITZ. Spray the paper with a light mist of water. You want it to be only slightly damp, not soaked.

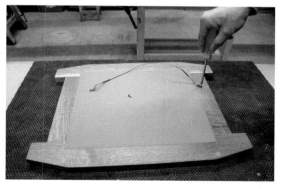

READY TO HANG. Attach a pair of screw eyes and picture wire to the back. If you wish, you can add plastic self-stick buttons (known as bumpers) to the bottom of the frame to keep the wood from hitting the wall.

3 ROUND-TOPPED TABOURET

The tabouret is a handy, versatile piece that can be used as a side table, nightstand, plant stand, or even a pedestal to display artwork. Slight changes in its height and the diameter of the top give you more options to adapt the piece to its surroundings. The designs of Gustav Stickley, from more than 100 years ago, inspired this tabouret. It features robust mortise-and-tenon joinery as well as a lap joint, which is very useful for connecting pieces that cross over one another.

In this chapter, I'll show you a simple way to make a perfectly round top; I'll also share a few tricks for gluing up panels that fit together perfectly and stay together with seasonal changes in humidity. And I'll show you a simple way to make thick-looking legs from thinner pieces.

Start at the Top

You're unlikely to find a single board wide enough to use for the top, so you'll need to join two or more boards edge to edge. The 18-in.-dia. top is one of the tabouret's prominent features, so make it from boards arranged both to show off the wood's figure or color and to remain flat

TABOUReT

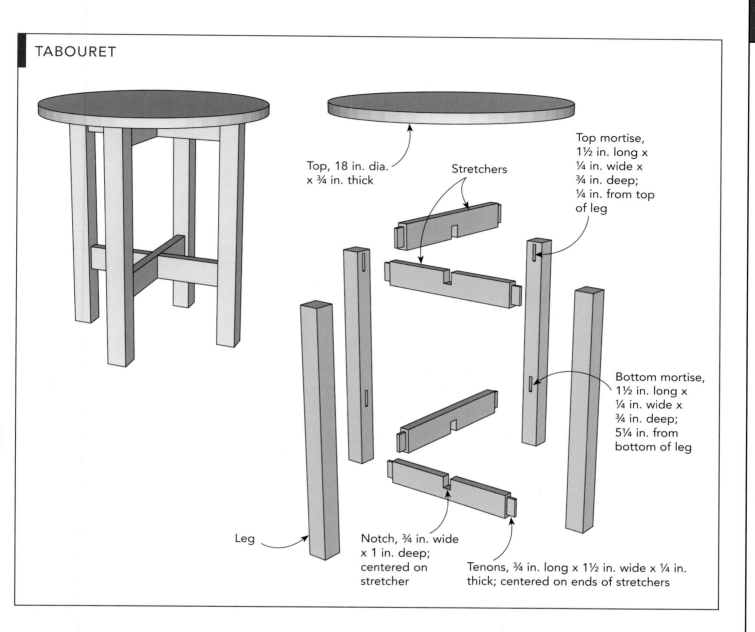

Top, 18 in. dia.
x ¾ in. thick

Stretchers

Top mortise,
1½ in. long x
¼ in. wide x
¾ in. deep;
¼ in. from top
of leg

Bottom mortise,
1½ in. long x
¼ in. wide x
¾ in. deep;
5¼ in. from
bottom of leg

Leg

Notch, ¾ in. wide
x 1 in. deep;
centered on
stretcher

Tenons, ¾ in. long x 1½ in. wide x ¼ in.
thick; centered on ends of stretchers

MATERIALS

QUANTITY	PART	THICKNESS*	WIDTH*	LENGTH*
4	Legs	1½	1½	19¼
4	Stretchers	¾	2	13
1	Top	¾	18	18

Total board feet: 3½

* Measurements are in inches.

MIND THE RINGS. When arranging the top boards, try to orient them so that the semicircular pattern of growth rings on the ends alternates direction—pointing up, then down, as shown.

GET A GOOD MATCH. Flip the boards for the top every which way until you get the grain and color match that looks best to you. Ideally, the grain should seem to blend smoothly from board to board.

and stable. I used quartersawn white oak for the table shown on these pages.

Cut the pieces for the top extra-long. I prefer to use an odd number of boards to help control seasonal wood movement. Once you have milled them flat and square (see chapter 2), spend time aligning them along their length until the figure and grain from adjacent boards seem to flow together. This will help camouflage the glue lines. If you choose to make this table from flat-

sawn oak or from another type of wood (cherry would be a nice choice), flip every other board over, so the growth rings visible on the ends alternately point up or down. This will help the finished top counteract (or at least average out) the wood's tendency to cup with seasonal changes in humidity.

Once you're satisfied with the arrangement of the boards, draw a triangle across them. This is known as a cabinetmaker's triangle, and it pre-

A large panel like this tabouret top is too wide for most jointers and planers. You need sweat and time to flatten it with a hand-plane. But you can save hours of hand work if you take the panel to a local cabinet and millwork shop. Most have a large machine called a wide-belt sander that can flatten and sand a panel in no time at all. The shop owners I know are happy to run panels through their sanders for a nominal fee.

KEEP THE BOARDS STRAIGHT. Use chalk to mark a large triangle across all the top boards. It will help you keep them in the proper order for glue-up.

vents you from mixing up the boards or getting them out of order.

Mill the edges of the boards again so that the edges fit together perfectly for a strong glue bond. You can do the final milling with a handplane or at the jointer. If you choose to handplane the edges, take two boards and put them face to face as if you're closing a book. Clamp the pieces edge-up in the bench vise, and plane both edges at once. It won't matter if the resulting edge is not exactly square to the faces; the planing creates complementary angles that add up to 180 degrees. So, when you open the book again, the boards will lie flat with no gap between them.

If you use a jointer, be sure its fence is square to the infeed and outfeed tables. To avoid even minor inaccuracies, mark an "I" on the face of one board and an "O" on the face of the other. Be sure the "I" face is "in" toward the fence while jointing that board and the "O" face is "out" away from the fence when jointing that edge. This accomplishes the same thing as jointing two boards at the same time with a handplane. When you bring the edges together, their angles will complement each other, resulting in a flat joint, even if your jointer's fence is way out of square.

PLANE IN PAIRS. If you handplane the edges of the top boards, plane them two at a time. Fold them together like a book when you clamp them in the vise.

COMPLEMENTARY ANGLES. Whether planed by hand or machine, the edges of mating boards will have complementary angles. (I've exaggerated the angles for the photo.)

MARK INS AND OUTS. If you use a jointer to finish the edges of the top boards, mark them as shown in the top photo. Edges marked with an I face toward the jointer fence. Edges with an O face away from the fence, as shown in the bottom photo.

GLUE UP THE PANEL

With the edges of the top smooth, flat, and square, you're ready to glue them up. For a panel this size, three clamps should suffice. Lay two clamps down and place the panel on them, using the cabinetmaker's triangle to keep the boards aligned. Apply a thin bead of glue on each edge and rub the boards together to help spread the glue. When all the boards are glued, position the top clamp in place and tighten it just enough to hold the panel together while you begin taking up the slack in the other clamps. With that done, work down the line of clamps, tightening them fully. Be sure the boards are all in the same plane and the edges are flush with one another. Allow the glue to cure overnight before working on or stressing the panel.

ASSEMBLE THE TOP. Rest the boards on the outside pair of clamps. Apply the glue and hold everything together with light pressure from the center clamp. Then tighten all three clamps firmly. I'm doing the glue-up on a scrap board placed on the tablesaw.

On panel glue-ups, the joint is long-grain-to-long-grain. When bonded with regular yellow glue, the resulting joint will be stronger than the wood surrounding it. There's no need for other wood or mechanical fasteners, such as biscuits or dowels.

Use a sacrificial piece of plywood or medium-density fiberboard (MDF) when you do glue-ups or apply finishes. Put the sacrificial piece on the tablesaw. That helps keep your tools and bench clean and provides some extra workspace.

Make the Thick Legs

It's usually pretty easy to find 4/4 lumber; for the most part, 8/4 lumber is also easy to obtain. But sometimes thick stock can be scarce or prohibitively expensive. The good news is, if you can't find thick stock for the legs, you can make your own. Take two ¾-in.-thick boards and glue their faces together to make a billet 1½ in. thick. This is another long-grain-to-long-grain joint, which is incredibly strong. You don't need to be concerned about it failing.

Avoid the mistake of cutting the two boards to the exact width you need. Aligning them perfectly during glue-up would be a challenge. Instead, cut them slightly oversize in width and length. After the glue cures, mill them to their final size of 1½ in. square and 19¼ in. long. Also, pay close attention to the figure of the wood at the glue line. Try to match two similar figure types, to make the joint as inconspicuous as possible.

Cut the Mortises and Tenons

Once you have cut the legs to size, move on to laying out and cutting the mortise-and-tenon joints. Each leg has two mortises, one for the stretchers that support the top, one for the lower pair of stretchers. The mortises are ¼ in. wide, 1½ in. long, and ¾ in. deep. Make them essentially the same way you cut the mortises

EASY THICK LEGS. Glue together two pieces of thin stock to make one thick leg. Cut the pieces oversize, then mill them to the final dimensions after the glue dries.

for the frame in chapter 2: Lay out the mortise location, drill out most of the waste, and chisel to the layout lines.

Cut the tenons the same way you cut them for the frame. Lay out the tenons, saw to the lines, and refine the fit with a rabbeting block plane.

Saw and Chisel the Lap Joints

Fitting stretchers into the legs creates two assemblies that need to be joined together. That's where the lap joint (or, more precisely for this situation, the half-lap joint) comes in. It is essentially a pair of matched notches.

To lay out the half-lap joint, find the center of each stretcher. Working from the centerline toward one end, measure half the thickness of one of the stretchers. Scribe a line with a marking knife to locate one side of the lap joint. Then put a piece of the actual stretcher against the scribed line and use it to mark the opposite side of the joint. Accuracy is paramount, so the finished joint will be centered on the stretcher and good and tight.

Using the marking knife and a combination square, continue the layout lines down the face of the stretcher. Then measure and mark half the height of the stretcher to identify the floor of the half-lap joint. Repeat for each of the four stretchers. Mark an X in the waste area for each piece, to ensure that you don't cut away the wrong part of the joint.

To finish the joint, remove the wood from the top to the half-way mark on one stretcher and from the bottom up to the half-way mark on the mating stretcher. The easiest way to do that is to saw to the half-way point, following the shoulder lines, using a handsaw designed for crosscutting. Then use a sharp chisel to quickly remove the waste.

Test-fit the joint. The rails should slide together and come apart with hand pressure alone. If the joint is too tight, you can use a wide chisel to pare away minute amounts of material from the shoulders until the fit is perfect. However, it's easier to take a pass or two with a plane on the face of the adjoining piece. No one will ever notice that one rail is a hair thinner than the other.

BEGIN MARKING THE HALF-LAP JOINT. Use a square and a marking knife to mark one side of the joint in each stretcher.

FINISH MARKING THE JOINT. Set another stretcher against the knife line and mark the opposite side of the joint. This is faster and more accurate than measuring the width of the joint.

THE FINAL MARK-UP. Once you've marked the sides and end of the half-lap joint, mark the part to be cut away to ensure you cut on the proper side of the line.

REFINE THE FIT. If the joint is tight, lightly plane both faces of one stretcher. That's much easier than trying to widen the notch in the board.

WORK SAFE

Routers are noisy, powerful little machines. At full speed, a router bit can spin at 25,000 rpm or more—twice the speed at which a race car's engine would explode! Always wear hearing protection and safety glasses whenever you are in the vicinity of a router.

VERSATILE BUSHINGS. These brass inserts fit around the bit and make it easy to guide the router when cutting shapes like the circular tabouret top.

Cut the Top Round

Remove the top from the clamps and spend some time with a scraper, plane, or sander to remove any glue squeeze-out and make the panel smooth and flat. There are several ways to create the circular top. The one I prefer involves a plunge router fitted with a ¼-in. spiral upcut bit and a ⅝-in. outside diameter guide bushing, used with a shop-made trammel.

The trammel is just a long scrap of ½-in. plywood wide enough to support the router. It has a small hole for a nail or screw at one end and a larger hole, sized to accommodate the guide bushing, at the other. The distance between the centers of those two holes (minus half the bit diameter) is the radius of the tabouret's top. To make the trammel, mark a line along its length and a shorter line to mark the center of the hole for the guide bushing. Use a Forstner bit to drill a hole for the bushing. Then measure from the short centerline to locate the position of the small screw hole.

CIRCLE-CUTTING TRAMMEL

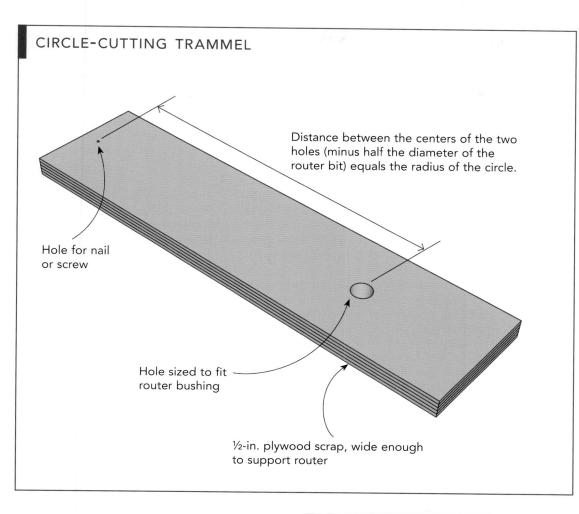

Hole for nail
or screw

Distance between the centers of the two
holes (minus half the diameter of the
router bit) equals the radius of the circle.

Hole sized to fit
router bushing

½-in. plywood scrap, wide enough
to support router

SIMPLE CIRCLE-CUTTER. The trammel
is a piece of scrap,
longer than the radius
you want to cut and
wide enough to sup-
port the router. A hole
in one end holds a nail
or screw on the center-
point on the top; the
larger hole, drilled at
the desired radius,
is for the guide bush-
ing attached to the
router base.

Work on the bottom face of the panel. Find
its center, then screw the trammel to the centerpoint. Don't make the screw too tight; the trammel needs to be able to turn. And don't worry
about the screw hole; the top stretchers will
hide it.

Cutting the circle will create a lot of dust and
chips, so be sure you have good dust collection
hooked up to the router. To protect the bench-
top, put some scrap under the workpiece; I use
scraps of plywood. Set the router for a ¼-in.
depth of cut. Make your first 360-degree pass,
moving the router counter-clockwise. As you
move the router around in a circle, you're likely
to hear two distinct cutting sounds (even if
you're wearing hearing protection): One is a con-

FIND THE CENTER. With a long ruler or straightedge, draw diagonals from corner to corner to find the center of the top piece.

ROUND AND ROUND. Attach the trammel to the centerpoint and insert the router bushing into its hole. Then make a series of shallow cuts, moving the router counter-clockwise, to cut the circle.

sistent buzzing, the sign of a good-quality cut. The other will be choppy and erratic; this indicates that the cut is shocking the bit and may break it. If you're hearing more of that choppy noise, try altering your feed speed until you get that nice even buzzing sound.

After one complete rotation, set the router to cut about ¼ in. deeper. At the end of your last pass, you will completely separate the top from the surrounding waste. Because the trammel is screwed to the top, there's little chance of the bit digging into the edge of the finished top and damaging it. However, you need to be careful not to bump the free-floating waste into the router bit as it slows down; the bit will grab into the waste and the bit could break. Or, the bit could jam against the waste, skip out of the trammel, and damage the good top.

To wrap up construction, you'll need a way to connect the top to the base. On the bottom edge of each upper stretcher, bore two ¼-in.-deep holes with a ⅜-in. Forstner bit. To locate the holes, split the distance between the half-lap joint and the tenon. Follow up by drilling through the stretcher completely, using a standard twist drill bit. A ⅛-in. bit will provide plenty of clearance for a #6 screw. Once you've drilled though, lever the drill back and forth in line with the length of the stretcher. This enlarges the hole, providing some room for the screws to move as the top expands and contracts.

Put It All Together

Dry-fit the tabouret to become familiar with the sequence to follow during glue-up. The tabouret goes together like a puzzle. Assemble the half-lap joints first, then fit the tenons into the mortises. I don't bother to glue the half-laps; they form a short-grain-to-long-grain joint, which isn't very strong. The mortise-and-tenon joints will hold this small piece together just fine. It's important that the top stretcher assembly sits flat and level and supports the top. I make sure the upper stretchers are aligned with the tops of the legs, to fully support the tabouret's top.

After the glued-up legs and stretchers have cured overnight, remove the clamps and prepare to secure the assembly to the top. To center the base on the top, draw a circle the same diameter as the width of the leg assemblies, using the small hole from the trammel as a centerpoint. Then line the base up with the circle and drive screws through the holes in the upper stretchers. Use screws that are long enough to bite into the top but not so long that they poke through (not that I've ever made that mistake!).

To finish the tabouret, check it for level by setting it on a dead flat surface; I use my table-saw. If the tabouret base wiggles or rocks, sand away a little material from the bottom of the longer leg or legs until the table is stable.

SMACK IT HOME. Fit each pair of stretchers together, then slide the legs onto the tenons. Use the heel of your hand to seat the tenons completely.

GLUE THE TENONS. Squeeze a small amount of glue onto the wide tenon cheeks and in the mortises. Don't glue the half-lap joints.

KEEP THINGS CENTERED. Draw a circle on the underside of the top and use it as a guide to center the base. Once it's in position, screw the base in place.

4 BOOKCASE WITH TUSK TENONS

This deceptively simple bookcase features many hallmarks of the Stickley style of American Arts & Crafts. Through-tenons—secured by tusks, or wedges—add to the styling and grab your attention, while contributing to the overall strength of the piece. I make my version of this classic with adjustable shelves, which adds versatility. The bookcase also throws a few curves at you: the arch at the bottom of the side panels and the rounded corner on the top of the sides. Both details are easy.

As you build this piece, you'll utilize many of the skills learned up to now as well as some new techniques: cutting mortise-and-tenon joints with a router, adding tusks to lock the tenons in place, and creating shiplap paneling for the back.

Make Plenty of Planks

This bookcase basically consists of a bunch of planks. Some are narrow and can be ripped from stock on the tablesaw, but most consist of narrow boards glued to make 12-in.-wide planks.

The bookcase plan and materials list show seven wide planks in all: three adjustable shelves, the top and bottom, and the sides. You

BOOKCASE WITH TUSK TENONS

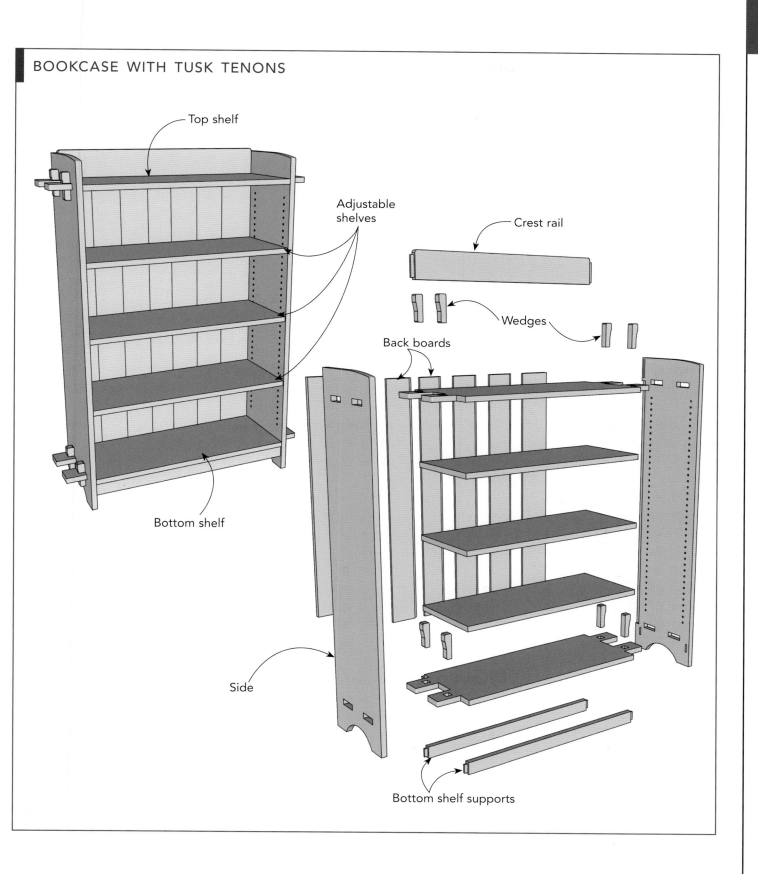

Top shelf

Adjustable shelves

Crest rail

Wedges

Back boards

Bottom shelf

Side

Bottom shelf supports

MATERIALS

QUANTITY	PART	THICKNESS*	WIDTH*	LENGTH*
2	Sides	¾	12	48
2	Top/bottom shelf	¾	12	35½
3	Adjustable shelves	¾	11⅛	28⁷⁄₁₆
2	Bottom shelf supports	¾	1¾	29½
1	Center back board	¾	4	40⅜
2	End back boards	¾	5	40⅜
4	Intermediate back boards	¾	4½	40⅜
1	Crest rail	¾	3¾	29½
8	Wedges	⅞	1	3½

Total board feet: 22

* Measurements are in inches.

MIX AND MATCH. Rearrange the boards for the sides and shelves until you find combinations that yield the best grain match.

can add more shelves or take some away, depending on the size of your library or the number of knickknacks you plan to place on them. Begin with two or more narrow boards for each shelf and side.

Mill the stock slightly fatter than the finished thickness of ¾ in., then flip the boards around until you find the best grain match for each pair. Use yellow glue to join the boards, just the way you glued up the top for the tabouret, in chapter 3. Clamp the boards and allow them to cure for at least an hour, preferably overnight. I usually use the curing time to select and mill the remaining components.

Once the glue has cured, scrape off any squeeze-out and run the boards through the planer. Remove minimal material from one face and then the other. This will help keep the boards flat. Plane until the planks are a consistent and uniform thickness. Rip them to width and crosscut them to length. I prefer to cut big planks to length on the tablesaw with a crosscut sled, or with a portable track-guided saw (see the sidebar at right).

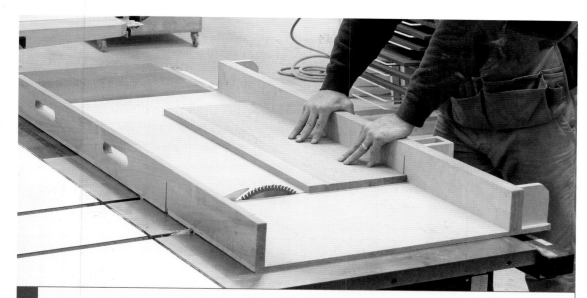

GO SLEDDING. A large crosscut sled, which rides in the tablesaw's miter gauge slots, is the safest for crosscutting pieces. You can clamp a stop block to the rear fence to cut multiple pieces to the same length.

How to Cut Long Pieces Safely

Long, wide planks like the ones for this bookcase can be a challenge to cut to length safely. They're generally too long for the miter gauge on a tablesaw and too wide for the typical sliding miter saw. When I need to cut boards like these to a consistent or critical length, I do it safely with a crosscut sled on the tablesaw.

You can buy a crosscut sled, but it's easy enough to make your own. It consists of a large platform and fences that register the workpiece and allow you to move it safely into the blade. A pair of runners on the bottom of the platform fit into the saw table's miter slots to guide the sled. You can clamp a stop block on the fence closest to the front of the saw for repeat cuts. There are countless articles in print and online describing how to make the crosscut sled. Google "Paolini Crosscut Sled" and you will find my video showing how to make one.

An alternative to the crosscut sled is the track saw. It's simply a circular saw guided by a precision track resting on the workpiece. There are several models readily available, all of which are more precise than an ordinary circular saw and a clamp-on edge guide.

Congratulations! Other than sanding and finishing, the adjustable shelves are done. (I tend to need that instant gratification.) However, there's still work to do on the top, base, and sides.

Start with the Sides

Rather than chop all eight through-mortises in the side panels by hand, you're better off using a router. It's really easy to cut them with a plunge router fitted with an edge guide.

LAY OUT AND CUT THE THROUGH-MORTISES

Use a pencil and combination square to lay out the location of the four mortises in each side panel. Then set up the router with a ½-in.-dia. spiral upcut bit and an edge guide. Position the guide so the bit lines up with one long side of a mortise. Cut one side of the two through-mortises at the top of the side panels, taking several passes and going only about ¼ in. deep at each pass to avoid stressing or breaking the bit.

Be sure to put a backer board underneath the side panel to help control any tearout from the spinning bit and to protect the workbench. Once you have made the first set of cuts, reposition the edge guide and cut the mortises to full width. This series of cuts will go quickly because you're cutting less material in each pass. Repeat the process for the mortises at the bottom of the side panel.

The routed mortises have rounded edges, so you need to square them up with a chisel. This part of the assembly is not very different from

SIDE PANEL, SHELVES, AND TRIM PIECES

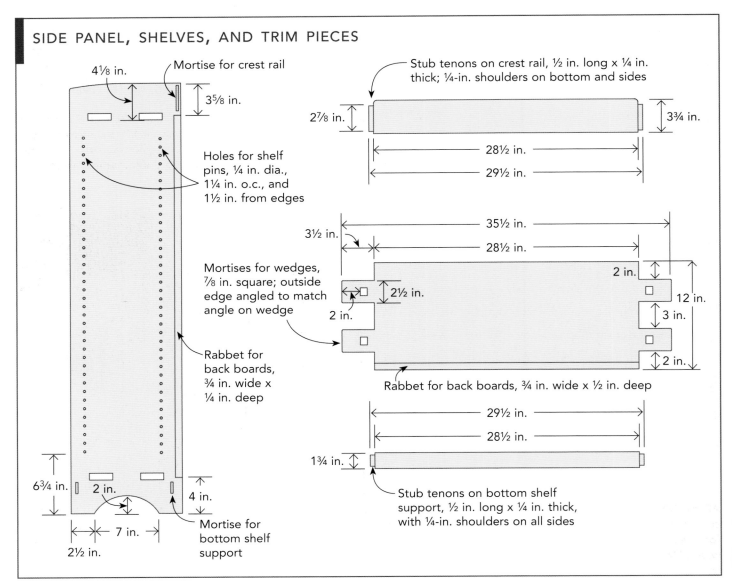

4⅛ in.

Mortise for crest rail

3⅝ in.

Holes for shelf pins, ¼ in. dia., 1¼ in. o.c., and 1½ in. from edges

Mortises for wedges, ⅞ in. square; outside edge angled to match angle on wedge

Rabbet for back boards, ¾ in. wide x ¼ in. deep

6¾ in.   2 in.   4 in.

7 in.

2½ in.

Mortise for bottom shelf support

Stub tenons on crest rail, ½ in. long x ¼ in. thick; ¼-in. shoulders on bottom and sides

2⅞ in.   3¾ in.

28½ in.

29½ in.

3½ in.   35½ in.

28½ in.

2 in.

2½ in.

2 in.

12 in.

3 in.

2 in.

Rabbet for back boards, ¾ in. wide x ½ in. deep

29½ in.

28½ in.

1¾ in.

Stub tenons on bottom shelf support, ½ in. long x ¼ in. thick, with ¼-in. shoulders on all sides cleaning up the mortises made with a drill press in earlier projects. This time, you only have to work on the ends, not the entire sidewall.

CUT MORTISES FOR THE TRIM PIECES

The sides have two ½-in.-deep mortises near the bottom for the bottom shelf supports and a similar mortise near the top for the crest rail. These mortises serve simply to position those trim pieces. Use a plunge router and a ¼-in.-dia. spiral upcut bit to cut these mortises. Make two plunge cuts to the full depth at each end of the mortise, then clear out the waste in between with multiple shallow passes. Square up the ends with a chisel.

LAY OUT MORTISES. Use a pencil and a combination square to outline the four through-mortises in each side piece.

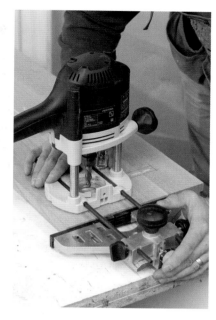

SET UP THE ROUTER. Position the router so the bit is flush with one side of the mortise. Attach an edge guide so the router follows the guide lines.

AFTER ONE PASS. When you've made the first cut for one set of mortises, reset the edge guide for a second cut to make the mortise its full width. Move the router from left to right to avoid making a climb cut.

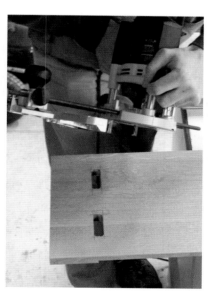

FINAL CUTS. These mortises are nearly complete.

CLEAN UP. Use a chisel to square the ends of the mortises. You don't have to do anything to the long sides.

SIDE PANEL DETAILS

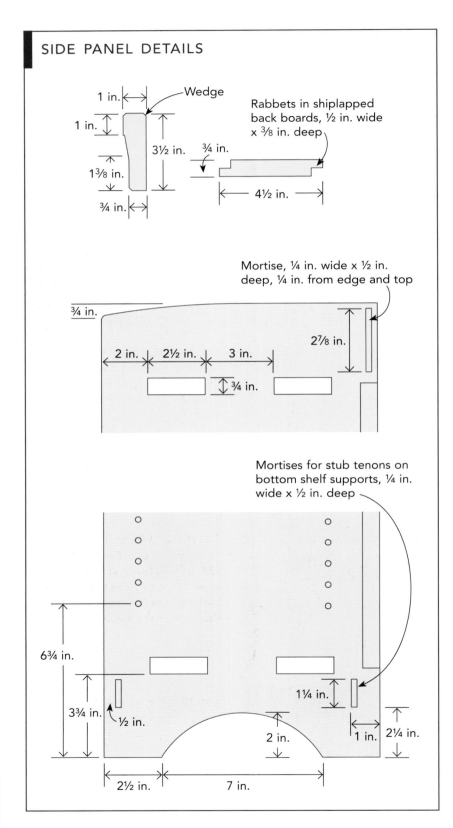

1 in.

Wedge

1 in.

3½ in.

¾ in.

1⅜ in.

¾ in.

Rabbets in shiplapped back boards, ½ in. wide x ⅜ in. deep

4½ in.

Mortise, ¼ in. wide x ½ in. deep, ¼ in. from edge and top

¾ in.

2⅞ in.

2 in.   2½ in.   3 in.

¾ in.

Mortises for stub tenons on bottom shelf supports, ¼ in. wide x ½ in. deep

6¾ in.

3¾ in.   ½ in.

1¼ in.

2 in.

1 in.   2¼ in.

2½ in.   7 in.

MORE SMALL MORTISES. Use a router to cut the smaller mortises for three trim pieces, then square their ends with a narrow chisel.

DRILL HOLES FOR THE SHELF SUPPORTS

A router can make a pretty efficient drill press, provided you have a way to keep the router perfectly steady. I do that with a simple jig made from ½-in. plywood. At the drill press, I painstakingly lay out and drill a line of equally spaced ⅝-in.-dia. holes in the plywood. Precision here is critical, so take your time with the layout and drilling.

Once I've made the jig, I label the top and bottom, clamp it to my workpiece, and use it to drill a line of holes for my adjustable shelf pins. I fit the router with a ⅝-in. guide bushing and a ¼-in.-dia. spiral upcut bit. Just slide the bushing into the hole in the jig, then plunge the bit to make the hole. Set the depth of the plunge to about ⅜ in., which will allow plenty of clearance for the shelf pins.

Whenever I use this jig, I'm guaranteed that the spacing of the holes will be exactly the same, provided I align the top or bottom edge as a reference to keep the holes in plane. I don't have to worry about my shelves being crooked or wobbly, even if the holes are not perfectly spaced center to center. Any errors in spacing will be duplicated in the other arrays in the

DRILL A SHELF-PIN JIG. Work carefully at the drill press to make an evenly spaced series of holes in a piece of plywood.

WORK SMART

If you'd prefer not to make a jig for the shelf-support holes, you have some alternatives: Use a piece of pegboard as a jig, drilling through its holes. Woodworking retailers also sell ready-made jigs, which are accurate but expensive.

project. Consistency is much more important than accuracy here.

CUT A RABBET FOR THE BACK

Follow the measurements on the plan on p. 36 to cut a rabbet on the inside back edge of each side piece. The rabbet will house the back boards. Use a bearing-guided rabbeting bit for this cut, and make the rabbet in two or three shallow passes. Because this is a stopped rabbet (one that does not extend the full length of the piece), use a chisel to square up the ends.

CUT THE CURVES

The curves on the top and bottom of the side panels are pretty straightforward. The simplest way to make them is with an electric jigsaw or a coping saw. Or you can use a bandsaw if you have one. Just follow the line using a fine-toothed blade in your saw. This will leave a cleaner edge that needs less cleanup. But even with the finest blade, you'll still have to do some smoothing. (If you think you'll make more than one of these bookcases, cut a template for the curves from a piece of ¼-in. plywood or medium-density fiberboard. That will save you some time

PIN-HOLE MAKER. Clamp the jig to the side piece. Outfit a router with a ⅝-in. bushing and a ¼-in. spiral upcut bit. Then just put the bushing in each hole and plunge the bit to make a hole.

RABBET FOR THE BACK. Use a router and chisel to make a stopped rabbet in the side pieces.

WORK
SMART

Most router bits and saw blades are made with carbide edges. Some bits, such as spiral bits, are usually solid carbide. Carbide is very sharp partly because it is very hard, and most very hard things tend to be brittle. Avoid over-stressing carbide bits when cutting, and always use care when moving them around. Accidentally bumping carbide against another hard object, such as a router body or saw arbor, can chip the carbide, effectively destroying it.

and ensure that the curves match from one case to the other.)

Cleaning up the sawn edge is known as fairing a curve. It's a term that boat builders use often. The process essentially involves taking down the facets of the edge to create a smooth transition from facet to facet. A convex edge like the roll-off on the top of the sides can be faired with a block plane or a sanding block with some coarse sandpaper.

Fairing a concave edge like the arc at the bottom of the sides requires different tools, the best being a spokeshave. It must be razor-sharp and well tuned in order to cut cleanly and effortlessly. Or you can use a sanding strip, which is just coarse adhesive-backed sandpaper mounted to a piece of wood about $1/16$ in. thick and a foot long. The strip is flexible enough to follow the curve but rigid enough that it won't dig in and sand just one spot. When you've faired the curve with the sanding strip, go in by hand and finish smoothing with progressively finer grits of sandpaper.

MASTER CURVE. For the arched cutout in the sides, make a template from thin plywood or MDF and trace the curve on the side panels. This ensures that both curves will be identical.

CUT CLOSE. Use a jigsaw to cut close to the line for the curve (left). Also use the jigsaw to cut the shallow curve at the top of each side piece (above).

ONE WAY TO FAIR THE CURVE. A well-tuned, razor-sharp spokeshave can quickly remove saw marks.

ANOTHER WAY TO FAIR THE CURVE. If you don't have a spokeshave, attach sandpaper to a thin wood strip to smooth the curve.

Shape the Top and Bottom Shelves

Cutting the long tenons on the ends of the top and bottom shelves, then chopping a mortise in each tenon for the tusk, is probably the most challenging part of the bookcase construction.

CUT THE TUSKED TENONS

Lay out the 3½-in.-long tusked tenons on the top and bottom shelves; also lay out the square mortises that hold the tusks. Adjust the router edge guide so that the bit just touches the line for the tenon shoulder. Position the router bit at the corner formed by the tenon cheek and shoulder, and plunge all the way through the wood. Later, square up the corners with a chisel.

With the edges of the tenons defined, make a series of shallow passes to define the tenon shoulders. Remove only ¼ in. of material at a time. Use a handheld ripsaw to cut the cheeks of the tenon. Clamp the workpiece in the bench vise or to the side of your bench and saw along the line.

You may wonder why the tusked tenons have to be so long, since the sides are only ¾ in. thick. When you drive the tusks in place, the force they exert can blow out the weak endgrain

TUSK TENON LAYOUT. With a pencil and a square, mark the position of the tusk tenons and the square mortises for the tusks on each end of the top and bottom pieces. Mark an X, as shown, in each area to be cut away.

DEFINE THE CORNERS. Use a plunge router to make a hole at each end of the tusk tenons.

CUT THE ENDS. Take a series of shallow passes with a router, fitted with an edge guide as shown, to make grooves connecting the routed holes. This defines the ends of the waste sections to be cut away.

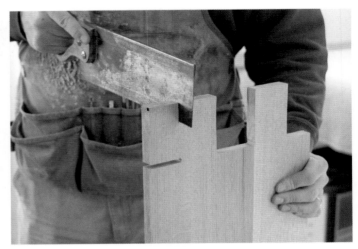

CUT AWAY. Use a saw meant for ripping to saw the cheeks of the tenons. Cut down to the routed slot.

at the end of the tenon. The length of the tenon ensures that there will be enough wood to withstand the pressure from the tusks.

CUT THE TUSK MORTISES

The easiest way to make the mortise for the tusk is to remove the bulk of the waste with a hand-held drill, then chisel to the lines to square up the opening. The mortise walls on the sides and the inside end are all straight and perpendicular to the face. The wall on the outside end is angled to match the shape of the tusk. You need to angle the chisel when cutting this mortise. You don't have to match the angle on the tusk

precisely; come as close as you can. You can also cut an angled block to guide the chisel.

ADD A RABBET

To finish off the top and bottom shelves, cut a rabbet for the back boards along one edge of each piece. You can cut this in one or two passes with a bearing-guided rabbeting bit, just as you did for the mirror frame in chapter 2, or you can use the edge guide and spiral upcut bit (which may still be set up in the router). Lay out the rabbet at $3/4$ in. wide and $1/2$ in. deep, then set the edge guide and router to remove this waste in multiple passes, adjusting the depth and edge guide as you go.

MAKE THE TRIM PIECES AND TUSKS

Cut the crest rail and the two bottom shelf supports to size. Lay out the stub tenons on the ends of each piece and cut them with handsaws. Round over the top edges of the crest rail.

To make the tusks, begin with a board that's about twice as wide and about twice as long as what you need for one tusk. Cut the blank on the diagonal from opposing corners, so you get

What's in a Name?

It's not hard to understand how the tusk tenon got its name: It resembles the long choppers that walruses, wild boars, and sabertooth tigers have. This type of joinery is said to date to the Middle Ages, but the "tusk tenon" name dates only to 1825.

DRILL FIRST. Begin shaping the mortises for the tusk tenons by drilling out most of the waste with a Forstner bit.

FINISH WITH A CHISEL. Use a wide chisel to finish shaping the mortises. Cut three sides straight down, but cut the last edge at an angle that's close to the angle on the tusk tenons.

two tusks from one board. Lay out the shape of a tusk in each triangle of wood (see the drawing on p. 38), then cut it out with a coping saw or bandsaw.

The angled face of the tusk should be roughly the same angle as the one on the through-tenon. You may have to tweak the angle a little bit with a block plane to get it just right. Slide the tusks into the mortises, locking the through-tenons in place. The tusks will most likely be at different heights, but that's easy to fix. Simply measure from the through-tenon, up a given amount, and then from the bottom of the through-tenon, down a given amount. Transfer this measurement to all of the tusks while they're installed in the tenons.

Remove the tusks and crosscut them to the marks you just laid out. Then reinstall the tusks, and you'll see that they're now all located at consistent heights.

RABBET THE SHELVES. Cut a rabbet for the back panels in the top and bottom shelves.

Create the Shiplap Panels

Shiplap is another term from the boatbuilding trade. A shiplapped board is rabbeted on opposite edges, so it's Z-shaped at the end.

TRIM THE TUSKS. To make all the tusks sit at a uniform height, measure up from the tenon a given amount, and down from the other side of the tenon by the same amount. Cut the tenons at those measurements.

When you lay the boards together, the rabbets overlap. The technique is how ships' hulls were covered to keep water out. Shiplapping also works well for covering the back of a carcase or cabinet piece. It's a little more refined than simply slapping on a piece of plywood.

The easiest way to cut shiplapped panels is on the router table. Chuck a straight cutting bit into the router. Adjust the height to a hair more than half the thickness of the board that you're going to mill. Set the fence back about 3/8 in. from the edge of the bit. Use a featherboard to put consistent downward pressure on the board. Move it from right to left to cut the rabbet. Flip the board over so the unrabbeted edge is against the fence and the freshly cut rabbet faces the ceiling. Cut the second rabbet. Repeat the process until you have enough boards to cover the back of the bookcase.

Put It All Together

One of the great things about this project is that there's no final glue-up. The back panels and tusk tenons hold everything together.

Do the assembly so that the front of the bookcase is against the bench. Slide the tenons in the top and bottom shelves into one side piece; be sure the rabbets in the two shelves face the ceiling and each other. Slip the tusk tenons into their mortises, and fit the crest rail and bottom shelf supports into their mortises. Then add the second side piece, fitting all the tenons into their mortises. Lightly tap all the tusk tenons to seat them firmly. Finish by screwing the shiplapped panels in place in the rabbets. Allow about a penny's thickness of spacing between the planks. Trim the excess off of the two end boards and screw the boards into the rabbets in the top and base. Now, if you unscrew the shiplapped panels, the entire bookcase can be knocked down for storage or shipping.

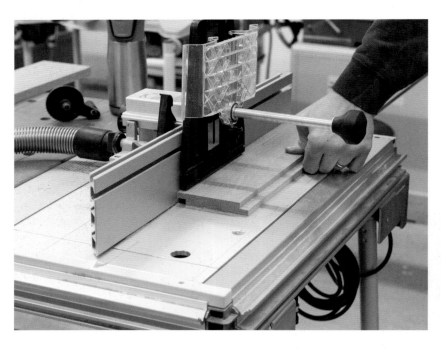

BACK PANEL RABBETS. To make the shiplapped back boards, cut rabbets on opposing ends and faces, as shown. It's easiest to make these cuts at a router table.

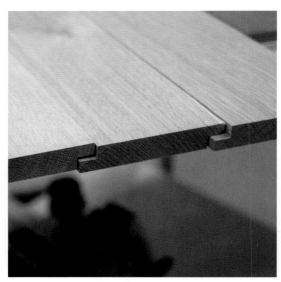

PANEL OVERLAP. The back boards overlap as shown. However, you'll have to cut away one rabbet on the boards at the ends.

FINAL ASSEMBLY. Slip the top and bottom shelves and the trim pieces in place, and hold everything together with the tusks. Check the case for square by measuring the diagonals, then screw the back panels into place.

PLACE THE SHELVES. Insert shelf pins into the appropriate holes and rest the adjustable shelves on the pins.

5 STICKLEY-INSPIRED SPINDLE BED

Beds are big, and they look more complex than they really are. Building one is a great project to help improve your skills as well as your confidence as a woodworker. This bed has a distinctive Arts & Crafts style, inspired by the work of the Stickley brothers. It's made of quartersawn white oak, but with longer and thicker boards than we have used for the projects in earlier chapters. If you can't procure suitably thick boards, you can utilize traditional Craftsman techniques to build up solid-looking pieces from thinner boards, as described below.

You can make the bed to fit any standard mattress, from twin to California king; the chart on p. 49 gives mattress sizes, which will help you scale the bed up or down. The rails attach to the headboard and footboard with sturdy hook-shaped hangers. They allow you to disassemble the bed so you can move it from workshop to bedroom.

SPINDLE BED

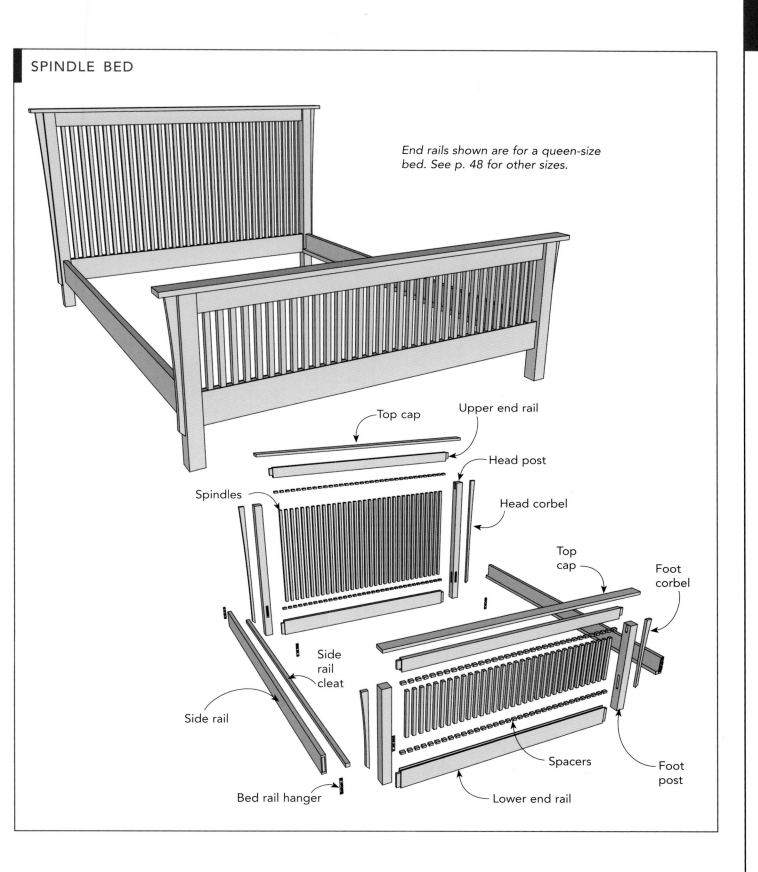

End rails shown are for a queen-size bed. See p. 48 for other sizes.

Top cap

Upper end rail

Head post

Spindles

Head corbel

Top cap

Foot corbel

Side rail cleat

Side rail

Spacers

Bed rail hanger

Lower end rail

Foot post

MATERIALS

QUANTITY	PART	THICKNESS*	WIDTH*	LENGTH*
2	Head posts	2¼	2¼	44
2	Foot posts	2¼	2¼	25
2	Upper end rails	1	3	61
2	Lower end rails	1	5	61
2	Side rails	1	5	80½
2	Side rail cleats	1	1	80½
33	Head spindles	¾	¾	31
33	Foot spindles	¾	¾	12
128	Spacers	½	¾	1
8	End spacers	½	¾	1⅛
2	Foot corbels	¾	1½	20
2	Head corbels	¾	1½	39
2	Top caps	¾	2¾	68½

Total Board Feet: 27½

HARDWARE

4	Bed rail hangers	

Note that end and side rails shown are for a queen-size bed. For other bed sizes, use these lengths:

   Twin: 40 in. end rails, 75½ in. side rails

   Full: 55 in. end rails, 75½ in. side rails

   King: 77 in. end rails, 80½ in. side rails

   California king: 73 in. end rails, 84½ in. side rails

You will also need to add or delete spindles and spacers accordingly.

* Measurements are in inches.

I'll cover a new way to make mortises in larger pieces like this. I'll also show you how to make the mortise-like joint to hold the numerous spindles in the headboard and footboard.

Start With a Careful Design

Design the bed around the mattress and box spring. The chart on the facing page gives standard sizes, but I have found that they can actually vary by an inch or two in length and width. So whether you're making a new frame for an existing mattress and box spring or plan to use new bedding, measure the box spring and size the frame accordingly. Allow an additional 1 in. to 1½ in. at the head and foot so you have room to tuck in sheets and blankets.

The height of the bed is less critical than its width and length. People are generally most comfortable with a seating surface between 18 in. and 24 in. from the floor. I use that same

TYPICAL MATTRESS DIMENSIONS

	LENGTH	WIDTH
Twin	75 in.	39 in.
Extra-long twin	80 in.	39 in.
Full	75 in.	54 in.
Queen	80 in.	60 in.
King	80 in.	76 in.
California King	84 in.	72 in.

range when designing a bed, because the bed is often used as a seat. However, there are no real standards for mattress thickness, so I've built beds with mattress heights that approach 36 in. The need to use the space under the bed for storage will also affect the mattress height. Be sure that you position the rails high enough so storage containers will fit under them.

One final design consideration: King mattress sets often use two twin-bed box springs, which require support down the center of the bed. Some queen sets also use a pair of box springs that need central support. This usually takes the form of a box or platform placed under the center of the bed.

Make Thick Pieces from Thin Stock

You'll need thicker stock for two key components of this bed. The rails are 1 in. thick; the posts, 2¼ in. square. You'll probably be able to find 5/4 stock and mill it to 1 in. thick for the rails. But the wood usually carries a premium price, so I laminate pieces of thinner stock together to make the long side rails as well as the shorter rails for the headboard and footboard.

LAMINATE THE RAILS

It doesn't matter if the seams for the rail laminations are centered, or if you glue pieces of equal thickness, as long as you end up with boards 1 in. thick. It's easiest to laminate two ¾-in.-thick boards and mill the resulting piece down. If you're fairly adept at resawing (see the sidebar on p. 50), you can glue up three pieces and cut the resulting 2¼-in.-thick piece in half at the bandsaw. Make the boards oversized in width and length, and cut them to size after you have finished the glue-up; this way you don't have to worry if the pieces shift slightly as you apply pressure with the clamps.

Let the glue cure overnight, scrape off the dried squeeze-out, and joint an edge flat and square. Plane it to final thickness. Since these pieces are long, I usually cut them to length at the miter saw. Consistency is much more important than accuracy here. The side rails must be identical in length. Likewise, the four rails for the footboard and headboard assemblies must be identical in length.

USE LOTS OF CLAMPS. Laminating thin pieces to make thicker stock for legs and rails requires lots of clamps. You may need to use all your clamps to glue one lamination at a time.

What is Resawing?

Resawing is a variation of rip-sawing, which means you cut the board along its grain, not across it. In a standard rip cut, you saw along the face of a board to create two narrower boards. In resawing, you cut along one narrow edge of a board to produce two thinner ones.

Resawing is usually done at the bandsaw, although I like to begin these cuts at the tablesaw. I cut two grooves down the center of each edge of the board. Then I use the grooves to help me steer the board at the bandsaw to finish the cut. A wide aggressive blade, with only 2 or 3 hook teeth per inch, works best for resawing. Feed the board into the bandsaw blade slowly. As you near the end of the cut, use a push stick or scrap block to move the board into the blade.

TRIED-AND-TRUE TECHNIQUE. Make the legs from a lamination of three thinner pieces, with thin veneers covering the seams. This is a classic Arts & Crafts technique to make thick pieces from thin stock.

LAMINATE THE POSTS

Make the posts from a lamination, too. This time, hide the glue seams with thin veneers. The finished leg will exhibit quartersawn figure on all four sides. That's something you won't find in nature, but it sure is pretty on a piece of furniture. This is actually a technique that Gustav Stickley and other Arts & Crafts cabinetmakers used in their furniture.

Begin by gluing up four sandwiches of three boards each, just as you did with the rails. Make the parts oversized in width and length. Let the glue cure overnight, then scrape off the excess. Joint one of the seamed faces flat, then plane the opposite face until the sandwich is 2 in. thick.

LAMINATION GLUE-UP. When gluing the veneers to the leg laminations, glue more than one leg at a time. The melamine-coated pieces surrounding the laminations are cauls that help spread the clamp pressure.

FIRST STAGE OF CLEAN-UP. Once the glue has dried, run two adjacent faces of each leg over the jointer. Then run the leg through a planer until it's 2¼ in. square.

For the veneers, find four boards with the grain and figure that look prettiest to you. Mill these boards to ¾-in. thickness. Resaw them to create eight pieces, each about ⅜ in. thick. Plane them to ¼ in. thick for the veneers.

Glue two veneers to each leg blank, covering the seams of the lamination. I use cauls to help distribute the clamping pressure onto the thin boards. Scrape off the excess glue and joint two adjacent faces flat and square. These will be your reference surfaces. At the planer, mill the leg to 2¼ in. square, using the jointed faces as reference. Pay particular attention to the veneered faces, making sure to remove equal amounts from each face for a consistent look. If any face needs some additional cleanup, do that with a flush-trim bit at the router table. The veneers should end up being ⅛ in. thick. If you ease the edges of the legs, the glue lines will virtually disappear.

Finish each leg blank by squaring one end and cutting the piece to length. Clamp a stop block to the saw fence to ensure that the posts

FINAL CLEAN-UP. Use a bearing-guided flush-trim bit at the router table for any final clean-up on the legs.

CUT TO LENGTH. At the tablesaw, trim one of the legs square. Flip it end for end and cut it to its final length. Clamp a stop block to the miter fence to ensure that the legs are identical in length.

WORK IN PAIRS. Lay out the location of the mortises in the headboard and footboard legs two at a time, to ensure that they match.

for the headboard are identical in length; the same goes for the footboard posts.

Make the Structural Joinery

The headboard and footboard are virtually the same, just with different heights. To avoid confusion and mixing up parts, I build the headboard and footboard separately. The process for creating them is identical, though.

You can create the joinery in one of two ways: With traditional mortise-and-tenon joints or with floating tenons. (For that joint, you cut an identical mortise in the two mating boards, then connect them with a third piece—the floating tenon—which is sized to fit the mortises.) The choice is strictly one of personal preference. The photos and plan show the traditional method.

USING TRADITIONAL MORTISE-AND-TENON JOINERY

Begin by determining the orientation of the legs and which faces will have mortises for the end rails. Place the legs on the workbench, joinery faces up, and begin laying out the mortises from a reference edge. I usually work from the bottom of the leg upward, but that's just my preference. Do the layout on two legs at a time to be sure that the mortises are in line with one another.

I think it's easiest to cut these mortises using a router fitted with an edge guide and a ½-in.-dia. spiral upcut bit. Cut the mortises to their 1-in. depth in a series of shallow passes. As the plan on the facing page shows, the mortises are 2 in. long for the upper end rails and 4 in. long for the lower end rails, centered on the face of the posts. Leave the ends rounded; there's no need to square them up.

POSTS, CORBELS, AND RAILS

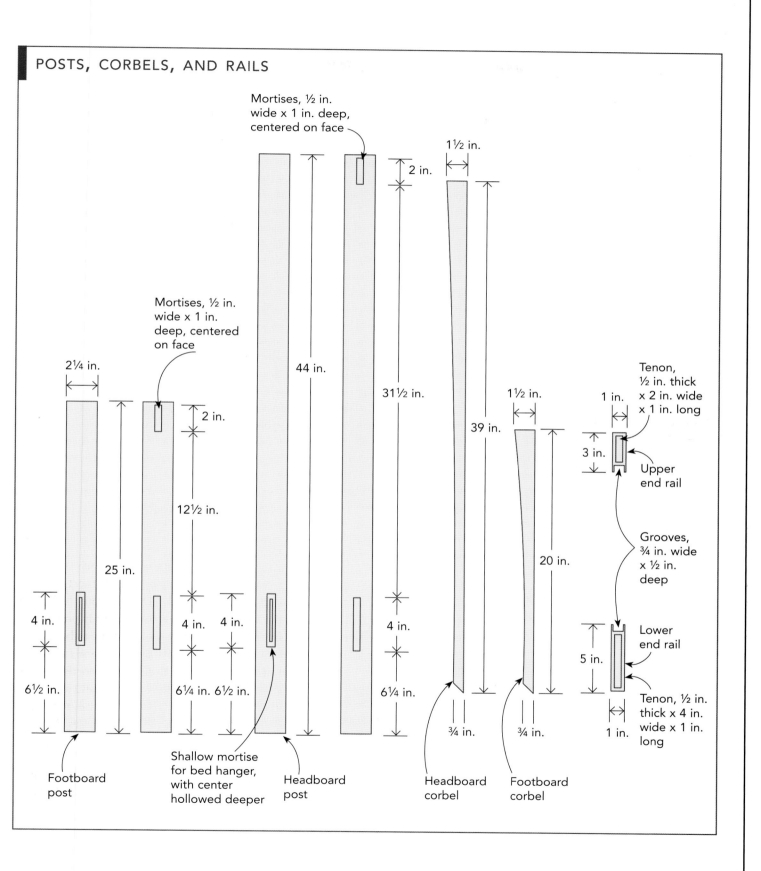

Mortises, ½ in. wide x 1 in. deep, centered on face

2 in.

1½ in.

Mortises, ½ in. wide x 1 in. deep, centered on face

2¼ in.

2 in.

44 in.

31½ in.

39 in.

1½ in.

Tenon, ½ in. thick x 2 in. wide x 1 in. long

1 in.

3 in.

Upper end rail

25 in.

12½ in.

20 in.

Grooves, ¾ in. wide x ½ in. deep

4 in.

4 in.

4 in.

4 in.

4 in.

5 in.

Lower end rail

6½ in.

6¼ in. 6½ in.

6¼ in.

¾ in.

¾ in.

1 in.

Tenon, ½ in. thick x 4 in. wide x 1 in. long

Footboard post

Shallow mortise for bed hanger, with center hollowed deeper

Headboard post

Headboard corbel

Footboard corbel

ROUT THE MORTISES. Use an edge guide to keep the router running true, and a spiral upcut bit to make the leg mortises. If you place the guide against the outside edge of one leg, be sure to place it against the outside edge of the other. If you don't, the mortises may not line up properly. Leave the ends rounded.

FILE TENONS TO FIT. Once you have cut tenons on the rails, use a file or rasp to round over the ends so they fit the mortises. The roundover doesn't have to fit the mortise exactly.

With the mortises finished, cut the tenons on the ends of the rails. You can do that with a handsaw (see chapter 2) or at the tablesaw. Once you've cut all the tenons, test their fit in the mortises and plane down any that seem too tight. When you can fit the tenons into the mortises without exerting too much pressure, use a rasp to round over the ends of the tenons so they will fit in the round ends of the mortises. The roundover doesn't have to be exact; the wide cheeks of the tenons do the bulk of the work to hold the joint together.

USING FLOATING TENONS

Cut mortises in the rails using the same router setup you used for the posts, but with the fence adjusted accordingly. Clamp thick scraps to each side of the rail to help support the router. If you're building a twin or full bed, you may be able to clamp the rails in the vise and work on them upright. For a queen or king bed, you will probably have to angle the rails and hold the router at an angle as well. In that case, practice on some inexpensive construction lumber until you're comfortable with the working arrangement.

At this point, you have a joint consisting of two mortises. That's not a mistake. Now, instead of sawing a tenon on one end of a board, cut a separate piece sized to fit in both mortises. A floating-tenon joint is virtually as strong as a traditional mortise and tenon. To create the floating tenons, plane a piece of oak to the thickness of the mortise, sneaking up on the size until the tenon fits the mortise snugly. Rip the piece to the width of the mortise. Round over the sides with a rasp or at the router table with a roundover bit. Cut the tenon to length—a hair shorter than double the depth of the mortise.

I like to dry-fit the assemblies at this point. I'm far from done, but seeing the assemblies together gives me enough gratification to keep going! Besides, it's nice to see if I messed anything up before continuing on (that's probably the real reason for the dry fit).

FIT A TENON. In floating-tenon joinery, you cut identical mortises in both members of the joint, then connect them with a separate tenon like the one shown here.

MORTISE THE RAILS. Cut a mortise in the end of each rail for the headboard and footboard, taking multiple passes until you reach the correct depth. Use an edge guide or clamp blocks to the side of the rails to steady the router for these cuts.

Add Decorative Joinery

The spindles that give this piece its signature look are purely decorative. You don't have to rout or chop dozens of mortises to house them; instead, the spindles fit in grooves in the end rails and are separated with spacers.

GROOVE THE RAILS

Begin by identifying which edges of the rails will be grooved. I draw a big chalk line on those edges. Then, using either a router outfitted with a ¾-in.-dia. spiral upcut bit or a dado blade mounted in the tablesaw, cut a ½-in.-deep

GROOVE THE RAILS. Use a router fitted with an edge guide to plow a groove for the spindles and spacers in the headboard and footboard. You can also use a dado set in the tablesaw to make the cut.

groove the length of the rails (see the drawing on p. 53). If you use the tablesaw, flip the boards end for end and make a second pass over the blade to ensure that the groove is centered. If you make the groove with a router, be consistent. That is, if the edge guide runs along the outside face of one rail, be sure you run the edge guide along the outside face of all four rails.

CUT THE SPACERS AND SPINDLES

Next, make a filler strip that is the same length, width, and depth as the groove you just cut. I begin cutting this piece on the tablesaw, but I prefer to finish milling it on the planer. Then, using a crosscut sled and a stop block at the tablesaw, cut a large collection of 1-in.-long spacer pieces; that's the distance between spindles. Cut as many spacers as you have spindles, and hang on to the remnants, which will be used for fillers at the ends of the rails.

Milling the spindles is straightforward but repetitive. Rough the pieces to width at the tablesaw, then use the planer to clean up the faces, making sure that the spindles are square. They should just slip into the groove in the rails. Finish by squaring an end and cutting the spindles to length. Save one of the offcuts for the next step.

SPACERS BY THE DOZEN. Once you've milled the filler strips for the headboard and footboard rails, cut each one into spacers that will fit between the spindles. The eraser end of a pencil makes a good tool for flicking each new spacer safely out of the way.

SPINDLES BY THE DOZEN. Rip the spindles from wider boards, then cut them to length.

ASSEMBLE THE SPINDLES

To assemble the spindles, do a dry fit in one rail. Begin by locating the center of the rail and position the offcut dead center. Position a spacer block against each side of the offcut. Continue to move the offcut and add a spacer block until you come close to the end of the rail. Determine how long a spacer you need at the end and cut four.

Glue the rails to one post, checking carefully to be sure the assembly is square. Glue the spacer blocks in at the ends of the rails, securing them with a drop of glue in the base of the groove. Slide in a spindle, then glue in a 1-in. spacer in each rail. Continue sliding in spindles and gluing spacer blocks until you reach the

When ripping the spindles from wider stock, it's easiest to set the saw's fence to the width of a spindle. Doing that can be dangerous because the narrow piece may kick back at you. To eliminate that danger, equip the saw with a splitter or a riving knife behind the blade.

opposite end of the rails. You could clamp each spacer block in place until the glue dries, but I prefer to tack them in place with an 18-gauge pneumatic brad nailer. The coarse grain of the oak does a great job of concealing the nail head.

Repeat the process on the remaining pair of rails. Once you have placed all the spindles and spacers, glue the remaining posts to the rails.

Attach the Embellishments

The headboard and footboard are embellished with top caps and corbels. The caps are plain pieces of ¾-in. oak. Rip them to width, cut them to length, and center them over the posts and top rails on the headboard and footboard. Attach them with a thin bead of glue.

ADD A POST. Once you have all the spindles and spacers in place, glue on the second post.

A DROP OF GLUE WILL DO. Hold the spacers in place with a small drop of glue. Don't glue the spindles. You can also use a 18-gauge nailer to tack these pieces in place.

SPINDLES AND SPACERS IN PLACE. Glue the rails to one post, then begin alternating a spacer and a spindle in the grooves in the rails.

GLUE ON THE CAP. Center the cap over the top rail and the posts, then glue it in place. Use plenty of clamps, and add blocks to protect the cap from the clamp jaws.

SHAPE THE CORBELS. Take the shape of the curve from the plan on p. 53 and make a pattern. Use the pattern to make a template for the router table, as shown here, or to make a cutting line for the bandsaw.

The corbels begin as square blanks, which ensures they will fit snugly between the posts and caps. Make a cardboard pattern for the corbel shape, trace the profile onto a blank, and cut it out either at the bandsaw or the router table. Clean up the rough-sawn edge with a sanding strip or a spokeshave. Or, if you have one, use an oscillating spindle sander. Attach the corbels to the posts with a thin bead of glue and clamp in place. (Use the waste as a clamping caul on the curved edge.)

Finally, attach cleats for the box spring to the side rails. These are 1-in.-square pieces of oak glued and screwed to the inner edge of each rail. Their mounting height should complement the height of the mattress and box spring you have selected for your bed.

ATTACH THE CORBELS. Glue these pieces in place, centering them on the posts. (Glue alone will be more than adequate to hold the corbels and caps in place.)

ADD CLEATS TO THE RAILS.
Hold the side rail cleats in place
with yellow glue and a few
wood screws.

Knock-Down Joinery

There are several types of hardware designed to
secure the bed rails to the headboard and
footboard and to come undone so the bed can
easily be moved. I prefer to use bedrail fasteners
that hook together. I screw the hook portion of
the connecter into a shallow mortise in the ends
of the rails; the plate that captures the hooks
screws into a shallow mortise on the posts.

Lay out the mortises on the post and side rail
(see p. 53). To make things easy, I chuck a bit in
the router that is the same diameter as the
width of the bedrail connecters; this allows
me to cut the mortise in one pass. I use the
connecter itself to set the router's depth of cut.
At the end, I square up the corners of the mortises with a chisel.

Notice that the hooks on the male part of the
connecter protrude through the back of the
mounting plate. You'll need to remove a little
wood from the rails to accommodate the protru-
sion. Place the plate in the mortise, and whack
the hooks with a hammer. That will leave a dent
in the wood showing exactly where you need to
remove material with a drill. Then drill a pilot
hole for a coarse-thread 4-in. screw to mount the
connecter into the rail. I use long coarse-thread

HANG-UPS. These sturdy connecters hold the
bed frame together and allow it to be
disassembled whenever the need arises.

ADD THE HANGERS. Shallow mortises in the
posts and the ends of the side rails house the
bed-hanger hardware.

MATCHING RECESSES. The posts and side rails each have a recess sized to fit the bed hanger hardware precisely.

SETTING BIT DEPTH. Use one of the bed hangers to set the cut for the mortise that houses the hardware. Here, I'm using a hanger to adjust the depth-stop on a plunge router.

WORK SAFE

Always unplug a power tool when making adjustments or changing bits or blades. On cordless tools, remove the battery for safety's sake.

MAKE ROOM. Plow a deep groove down the center of the shallow mortise on each post. The groove provides clearance for the hooks on the hanger that fits on the side rail.

screws for a good hold in the weak end grain in the rails.

Before attaching the plate to the post, you'll have to remove a little more wood to accommodate the hooks. I do that with a router. Without changing the edge-guide setting, I remove the bit I just used to cut the mortise and replace it with a ¼-in. spiral upcut bit. If you don't change the edge guide, the cut will be centered on the mortise. To locate this final cut, I trace the plate openings with a pencil and add the hook's extension. Set the depth of cut to be just a hair deeper than the distance the hooks protrude through the mating plate. You'll likely have to take multiple passes. Secure the plate with 1⅝-in. coarse-thread screws.

Final Assembly

Gluing up the headboard and footboard takes care of nearly all the assembly. So for twin and full beds the only thing left is to attach the rails to the headboard and footboard.

For queen and king beds you'll need to fabricate the center support. Measure the distance from the floor to the top of the end rail for the box spring. Use plywood or a secondary wood like poplar to make a box that height and about 6 in. wide. It should be the same length as the rails.

FRAME-AND-PANEL NIGHTSTAND

This simple nightstand could fit into several Arts & Crafts genres, but, as with many projects in this book, it originated with Gustav Stickley. Although it looks simple, the nightstand is packed with plenty of new opportunities to increase your woodworking skills. Its construction uses a variation of frame-and-panel joinery that is sometimes termed post and panel; that's because part of the framework serves as the posts, or legs, of the piece. The door and the drawer use different types of joinery. To make the panels for the sides, back, and door, you slice thin pieces from a thicker board and bookmatch them. You'll also learn how to install hinges and latches.

I used quartersawn white oak for the nightstand shown here, but the piece would look just as good if made from walnut or cherry.

Begin with Glue-Ups and Milling

You can mill most of the components from short, narrow boards, but you will need thicker or wider stock to make a few major components—the legs, top, and lower shelf. Glue up those panels, using the methods described in chapter 4,

(Continued on p. 64)

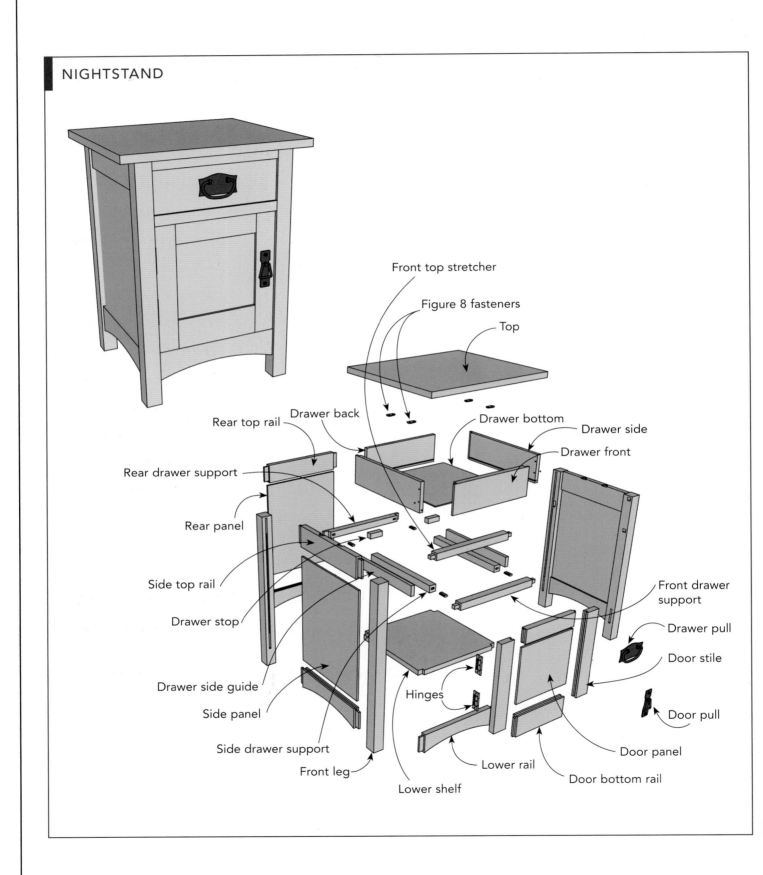

Front top stretcher

Figure 8 fasteners

Top

Drawer back

Drawer bottom

Drawer side

Drawer front

Rear top rail

Rear drawer support

Rear panel

Side top rail

Drawer stop

Drawer side guide

Side panel

Side drawer support

Front leg

Hinges

Lower shelf

Lower rail

Front drawer support

Drawer pull

Door stile

Door pull

Door panel

Door bottom rail

MATERIALS

QUANTITY	PART	THICKNESS*	WIDTH*	LENGTH*	MATERIAL
4	Legs	1½	1½	24	Quartersawn white oak
3	Side/rear top rails	¾	3	13½	Quartersawn white oak
3	Side/rear panels	¼	12½	16	Quartersawn white oak
4	Lower rails	¾	3	13½	Quartersawn white oak
1	Front top stretcher	1	1	13½	Quartersawn white oak
1	Front drawer support	1	1	13½	Quartersawn white oak
1	Rear drawer support	1	1	13½	Secondary wood
2	Side drawer supports	1	1	12¼	Secondary wood
2	Door stiles	¾	2	12½	Quartersawn white oak
1	Door top rail	¾	2	8½	Quartersawn white oak
1	Door bottom rail	¾	3	8½	Quartersawn white oak
1	Door panel	¼	8½	8	Quartersawn white oak
1	Drawer front	¾	4	12	Quartersawn white oak
2	Drawer sides	½	4	13	Secondary wood
1	Drawer back	½	4	11½	Secondary wood
1	Drawer bottom	⅛	12	12½	Plywood
2	Drawer stops	¾	¾	2	Secondary wood
2	Drawer side guides	½	1½	12	Secondary wood
1	Lower shelf	¾	13⅛	13½	Quartersawn white oak
1	Top	¾	16	18	Quartersawn white oak

Total Board Feet: 9

HARDWARE

QUANTITY	PART	THICKNESS*	WIDTH*	LENGTH*	MATERIAL
2	No-mortise hinges		¾	2½	
1	Bullet catch			7/16 dia.	
1	Drawer pull		1⅞	3⅝	
1	Door pull		1	3¾	
4	Figure 8 fasteners				

* Measurements are in inches.

ASSEMBLE THE TOP. Glue up narrower boards to make one wide panel for the top. Once the glue dries, rip it to width and cut it to length.

TRIM TENONS. Whether you use floating tenons or traditional mortise-and-tenon joinery as shown here, you'll probably need to plane the tenons so they fit the mortises snugly.

and either procure thick stock for the legs or laminate them from thinner pieces (see chapter 3). You'll cut and assemble the panels later, once you've finished the structural portion of the construction.

In previous chapters I showed you two ways to make mortise-and-tenon joints. Feel free to use whatever method you prefer to construct the nightstand. If you favor traditional mortise-and-tenon joinery (see p. 52), cut the pieces as shown in the drawings. If you lean toward floating tenons (see p. 54), omit the tenon lengths from the frame pieces.

Mill the legs and cut them to length. Plane, rip, and cut to length the upper side and rear rails, the lower rails, and the front top stretcher and front drawer support. Also begin milling the parts for the drawer and the door frame, but don't cut them to their final length yet; wait until you've finished the basic case.

Don't concern yourself at this point with the arch shape on the lower rails. Whenever possible, square up pieces and cut joinery before you add curves or other embellishments.

Lay Out the Structure

Determine the orientation of the legs, putting the faces with the best-looking grain and figure on the outside. Hold all four together and mark their tops with a cabinetmaker's triangle. Begin laying out horizontal lines for the mortises, following the measurements in the plan on the facing page. Work methodically: Mark the rear legs for the mortises for the rear rails first, then mark the front and rear legs for the mortises for the side rails, and so on. To make the layout easier, I gang the legs, aligning them at the bottom, and clamp them together. Then I use a square to carry the layout lines across all the legs at once.

When laying out the vertical lines, which will make up the mortise walls, be sure to reference opposite joints from the same plane. In other words, measure all the vertical lines from outside faces for consistency.

FRAME JOINERY

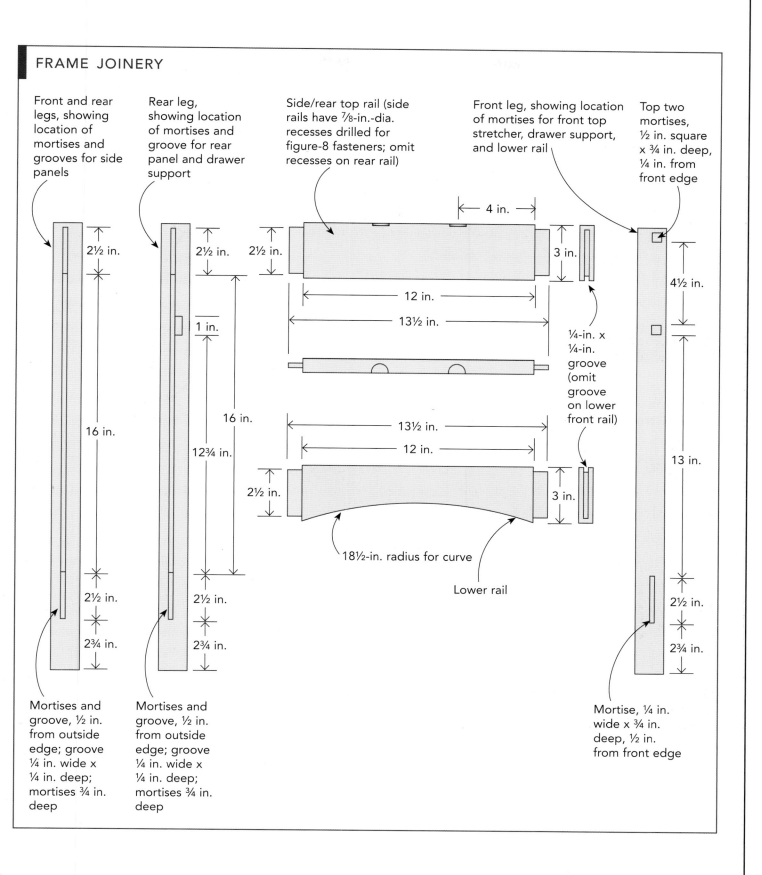

Front and rear legs, showing location of mortises and grooves for side panels

Rear leg, showing location of mortises and groove for rear panel and drawer support

Side/rear top rail (side rails have ⅞-in.-dia. recesses drilled for figure-8 fasteners; omit recesses on rear rail)

Front leg, showing location of mortises for front top stretcher, drawer support, and lower rail

Top two mortises, ½ in. square x ¾ in. deep, ¼ in. from front edge

2½ in.

2½ in.

2½ in.

4 in.

3 in.

4½ in.

16 in.

1 in.

16 in.

12¾ in.

12 in.

13½ in.

¼-in. x ¼-in. groove (omit groove on lower front rail)

13½ in.

12 in.

13 in.

2½ in.

3 in.

18½-in. radius for curve

Lower rail

2½ in.

2½ in.

2½ in.

2½ in.

2¾ in.

2¾ in.

2¾ in.

2¾ in.

Mortises and groove, ½ in. from outside edge; groove ¼ in. wide x ¼ in. deep; mortises ¾ in. deep

Mortises and groove, ½ in. from outside edge; groove ¼ in. wide x ¼ in. deep; mortises ¾ in. deep

Mortise, ¼ in. wide x ¾ in. deep, ½ in. from front edge

KEEP THEM STRAIGHT. Arrange the four legs so their best faces show, then mark them with a cabinetmaker's triangle so you can keep them properly oriented through construction.

BE CONSISTENT. When laying out mortises, always reference the marks from the same face. Here, I'm laying out the mortises for the front stretchers, working from the outside edge of the post. I'll work from the same edge to do the layout on the opposite post.

LAY OUT JOINTS SYSTEMATICALLY. Align pairs of legs and lay out the joints on both at the same time. Here, I'm marking the ends of mortises.

When you have finished the mortise layout, mark the tenons on the top and lower rails, the front stretcher, and the front drawer support. Once you have laid out all the joinery, cut the mortises and tenons using whatever method you prefer.

Once you have all the joints complete, do a dry fit to check your work. Adjust any joints if necessary for a good fit. This may involve shaving a tenon cheek to fit the mortise perfectly or trimming the shoulder to get a tight fit against the leg.

If everything looks good, use chalk to mark the inner edges of each frame piece, including the inner faces of the legs. Mark the inner edges on every face of the nightstand except the front. Disassemble the carcase. Use a router equipped with an edge guide and a ¼-in.-dia. spiral upcut bit to cut grooves in the rear legs and rails for the rear panel and the front and rear legs and side rails for the side panels. As you can see from the plan on p. 65, the grooves run the full length of the rails, and they run between the mortises on the legs.

WORK
SMART

Because of the size of the legs and the location of the mortises, adjacent mortises within a leg may cut into one another. That is completely normal and won't weaken the joints or the overall strength of the case.

CUT CONSISTENTLY. When routing the mortises, hold the edge guide against the same face on mating pieces, to ensure that the mortises will line up properly.

CHALK THEM UP. It will help you keep all the pieces organized if you mark the inside faces with chalk, and chalk a mark on the edge that will receive a groove.

DOING DOUBLE DUTY. Clamp three or four rails together, as shown here, when you rout the grooves on their edges. The extra boards help steady the router.

FIRST TEST. Dry-fit the legs and rails, making any needed adjustments, before moving on with the rest of the case assembly.

Make Bookmatched Panels

At this point, the nightstand looks more like a skeleton than a piece of furniture, but we will remedy that by creating bookmatched panels for the sides, back, and door. As the name implies, a bookmatched panel is created by resawing a board (see the photo at left) and opening the pieces like a book. The two halves are virtual mirror images and can be joined to form a single panel.

Since bookmatched panels are decorative, select boards with the most appealing grain and figure. The boards should be wider than half the width of the panel you'll need. Resaw the board and open it up to reveal the bookmatch. Keep in mind that you can open the match from either edge, so experiment until you get the best look. Mark the endgrain with letters or numbers to keep the pieces organized.

Head to the planer and bring the pieces down to their final 1/4-in. thickness. If you have a drum sander or a wide-belt sander, you can use it instead. Edge-glue the boards together and let them cure overnight. Thin panels like these will tend to spring out of the clamps if you apply too much pressure, so you may have to put additional clamps or cauls on the joint. Once the glue has cured, use a card scraper or a sander to flush the joints of the panel and remove excess glue. The panels are now ready to be cut to their final size.

CUT THE PANELS TO SIZE

Don't simply rip the bookmatched panels to width. Instead, make the cuts so the seam on the panel stays centered. Calculate the desired overall width of the panel, deduct about an 1/8 in. for expansion and contraction, divide that number in half, and measure that distance from the seam. Draw a tick mark, which will be the location for your first rip cut. Adjust the rip fence on your tablesaw until the blade is on the outside (waste) edge of the tick mark, and make the cut. Rotate the panel 180 degrees and set the rip fence to the desired overall width of the

SECOND SAWING.
Begin making the nightstand panels by resawing pieces. That is, stand a board on edge and cut it lengthwise at the bandsaw. Use a tall fence, as seen here, to steady the board.

AN OPEN BOOK.
Separate the resawn parts of the board as if you're opening a book. As you can see, the grain on one piece mirrors the other.

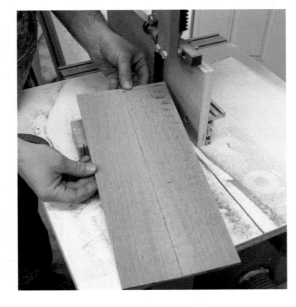

panel. Make the second cut. The panel should now be the proper width, and the seam should be dead center.

Cutting the panel to height is simpler. Square one end, using a crosscut sled on the tablesaw. Flip the piece around, and cut it to the desired height. You don't need to allow any room for expansion when cutting to height, because wood really doesn't expand or contract along its length.

After cutting all the panels to size, I like to do another dry fit. Dry fitting, even multiple times, is cheap insurance to make sure everything goes smoothly during final assembly and glue-up.

MEASURE THE PANELS. Measure from the glue line toward each side of the panels, so that the bookmatched grain pattern will remain centered.

SAW THE PANELS TO SIZE. Rip one side, flip the panel, reset the saw fence, and rip the second side. Use a crosscut sled in the tablesaw to cut the panel to its final height.

SECOND TEST. It's a good idea to do a second dry fit, clamping pieces together lightly, before you add a shelf and the drawer supports.

Move Inside

With the nightstand framework complete, it's time to cut and fit the lower shelf and add the drawer supports. Lightly clamp the dry-fit carcase together while you fit these pieces.

MAKE THE SHELF

Cutting the lower shelf to size is very straight-forward, but fitting it in place can be tricky. You may want to do a practice run with some scrap plywood before you move on to the white oak. The shelf rests on top of the lower rails and butts up against the inside faces of the side and rear panels. It's notched to fit around the legs.

The lower shelf should be oriented with the grain running from side to side, so that seasonal expansion will occur toward the front. The side-to-side dimension of the shelf should be the same as the distance between the side panels.

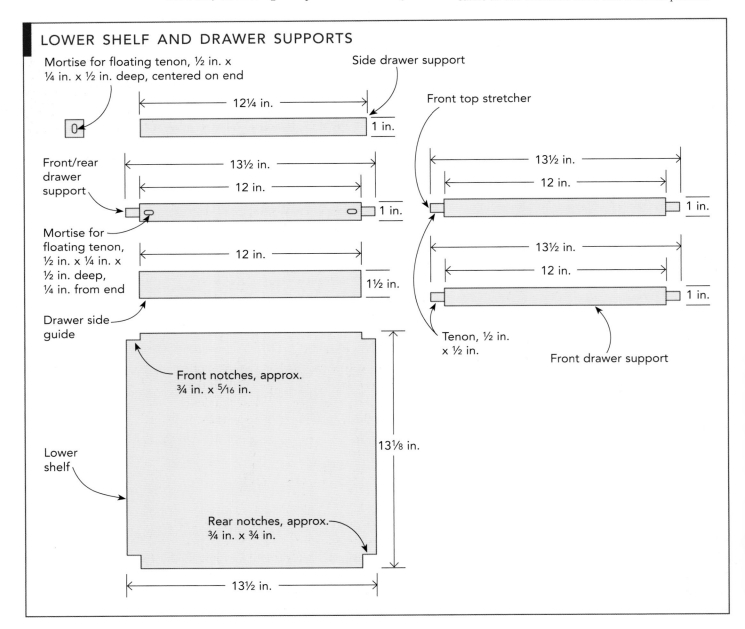

LOWER SHELF AND DRAWER SUPPORTS

Mortise for floating tenon, ½ in. x ¼ in. x ½ in. deep, centered on end

Side drawer support

Front top stretcher

12¼ in.

1 in.

13½ in.

12 in.

1 in.

Front/rear drawer support

13½ in.

12 in.

1 in.

Mortise for floating tenon, ½ in. x ¼ in. x ½ in. deep, ¼ in. from end

13½ in.

12 in.

1 in.

12 in.

1½ in.

Drawer side guide

Tenon, ½ in. x ½ in.

Front drawer support

Lower shelf

Front notches, approx. ¾ in. x 5/16 in.

13⅛ in.

Rear notches, approx. ¾ in. x ¾ in.

13½ in.

NOTCH THE SHELF. Use a bandsaw or a handsaw to notch the corners of the shelf so it fits around the legs.

Make this cut, using a crosscut sled at the table-saw. The front-to-back dimension is from the back panel to just ⅛ in. shy of the outside face of the front legs. Make this cut, again using a crosscut sled.

Next, make notches for the legs in the corners. Begin with the back legs, measuring how far the legs extend from the rear and side bookmatched panels. Transfer those measurements to the shelf and use a combination square to draw the leg location. Once you've laid out the notches for the back legs, repeat the process for the front legs.

Cut out the notches with a bandsaw or hand-saw. The cuts should be clean, but don't worry if they are not 100 percent perfect. The notches and edges need a little extra clearance, so you can insert the shelf into the nightstand vertically and turn it horizontally. It's impossible to get a glove-tight fit.

ADD THE DRAWER SUPPORTS

You already have the front portion of the drawer support mortised into the front legs of the nightstand, so you only need to add three more pieces. Because these supports will never be seen, you can make them from a secondary wood or less attractive pieces of oak.

FIT THE SHELF. Make the shelf a slightly loose fit so you can rotate it into position.

The rear support is a mirror image of the front one, as the plan on the facing page shows. The two side supports fit between the front and rear supports and are connected with mortise-and-tenon joinery. Floating tenons are great for this application, as you can cut the side supports to precise length.

Cut the mortises in the supports with a router, then shape floating tenons to fit; they are the same width and thickness as the mortises and twice the mortise depth. Dry-fit the drawer supports. Cut the side drawer guides to fit and glue them to the outer faces of the side supports.

Curve the Rails and Glue-Up the Case

Once all the case parts fit nice and tight, you can cut the curves on the lower rails. Cut the curve on the bandsaw and smooth the cut edge with sandpaper or a spokeshave (see chapter 4). Or make a template from a piece of ¼-in. plywood or medium-density fiberboard and use it with a router and bearing-guided router bit. After you've finished that last detail, you're ready to glue up the case. Here's the sequence I follow:

Glue up the rear assembly first: Put one rear leg on the workbench. Apply glue to one tenon on each rail and slip the rails into the mortises. Slide the back panel into its groove; don't use any glue on the panel. Apply glue to the tenons on the rails and slide the other rear leg onto the tenons. Clamp the assembly and check it for square. Cinch down on the clamps and let the assembly cure for at least an hour. Follow the same procedure to glue up the front legs and rails.

After the front and rear assemblies have cured for about an hour, finish the glue-up. Place the rear assembly on the workbench so the mortises for the side rails point toward the ceiling. Apply glue to the tenons on the side rails and slide them into the assembly. Do the same to fit the drawer supports into place. Slide the side panels in place, but don't use glue on them. Apply glue to the exposed tenons and fit the front assembly in place. Clamp everything and check it for square. Let the glue cure overnight.

Make the Door

The door's construction is essentially a variation of the post-and-panel joinery for the main carcase.

BEGIN WITH THE FRAME

The frame for the door is held together with stub-tenon joints. That is, a short tenon fits into a groove instead of a mortise. The groove also houses the door's center panel. A stub-tenon joint is not as strong as a conventional mortise-and-tenon or floating-tenon joint, but it is very easy to make and fine for a piece like this door. You can put pins through the stub tenons to increase the joint's strength if need be.

Begin by selecting, milling, and cutting to size the pieces for the door frame. Lay them out on the bench and determine their orientation. Mark the inner edge and outside face of each piece with chalk. Cut a groove that's ¼ in. wide and ¼ in. deep on the inner edge of all four frame pieces. I do this either with a dado blade in the tablesaw or with a router and an edge guide. If you cut the grooves with a router, make sure you always place the edge guide against the outside face of the frame, so the grooves are consistent. If you use a tablesaw, center the groove by making two passes, flipping the board after the first cut.

Move on to the tenons on the rails, or horizontal members. It's easiest to cut them at the tablesaw. Make multiple passes. Flip the board after each cut, so both faces have identical cuts. Raise the blade very slightly after each pair of cuts, to sneak up on a good fit.

ADD THE PANEL

Dry-fit the frame and lightly clamp it together. Check for square and measure the height and width of the opening. Add ½ in. to the height and ⅜ in. to the width. Cut the bookmatched panel to those dimensions, making sure to keep the seam centered.

Dry-fit the completed door again. Trim the height of the panel if necessary so that it fits

GROOVE THE DOOR FRAME. Cut a shallow groove in the door rails and stiles; the groove will hold the center panel and serve as a mortise for short tenons on the rails.

DOOR PARTS

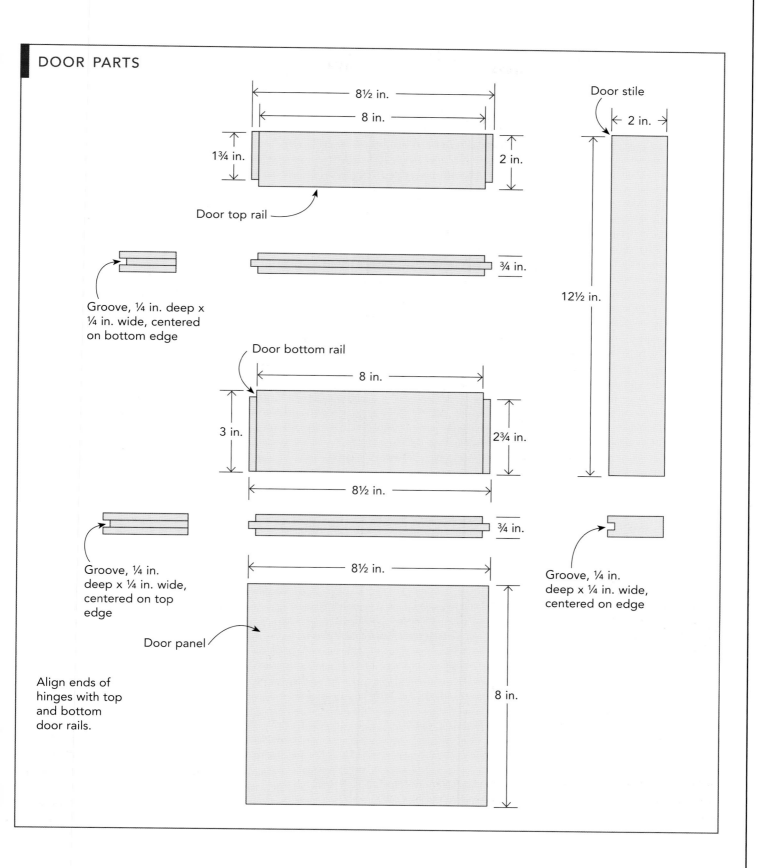

8½ in.

8 in.

1¾ in.

2 in.

Door top rail

Groove, ¼ in. deep x ¼ in. wide, centered on bottom edge

¾ in.

Door stile

2 in.

12½ in.

Door bottom rail

8 in.

3 in.

2¾ in.

8½ in.

Groove, ¼ in. deep x ¼ in. wide, centered on top edge

¾ in.

Groove, ¼ in. deep x ¼ in. wide, centered on edge

Door panel

8½ in.

8 in.

Align ends of hinges with top and bottom door rails.

CUT STUB TENONS.
Make multiple passes at the tablesaw to cut these short tenons. Raise the blade after each pair of cuts until the tenon fits easily in the groove.

THIRD TEST.
Assemble the door frame and panel to check the fit prior to glue-up.

DOOR GLUE-UP. If everything checks out in the dry fit, glue the door together. Don't get glue on the panel, though, because it needs to be free to expand and contract with seasonal changes in humidity.

WORK SMART

When fitting a stub tenon, it's easy to force the groove open and even split the wood. A properly cut stub tenon should fit with fairly light pressure. It shouldn't take the same force that a traditional tenon requires.

snugly but not too tightly. When everything seems all right, glue the stub tenons into the grooves. Don't glue the panel in place. Clamp the door tight, check it for square, and let the glue cure overnight.

Build the Drawer

Drawers are often assembled with dovetail joints. For this piece, however, I use a simple but strong joint known as a pinned rabbet. Of course, you can substitute dovetails if you wish; see chapter 7 for a simple way to make dovetails at the tablesaw.

MILL THE PARTS CLOSE TO SIZE

Select a nicely figured piece of quartersawn white oak for the drawer front. You can use a secondary wood for the sides and back. The bottom is made from 1/8-in. plywood. Plane everything but the bottom panel to final thicknesses, but leave the pieces slightly oversized in width and length. You'll fine-tune the fit with handplanes to fit the drawer opening precisely.

CUT SOME RABBETS AND GROOVES

Begin with the drawer front. Trim it to be about 1/16 in. narrower than the opening in the carcase. Plane it so that its width is about 1/16 in. less than the height of the opening, which will allow for seasonal wood movement. With a dado blade in the tablesaw, cut a rabbet in each end of the

DRAWER PARTS

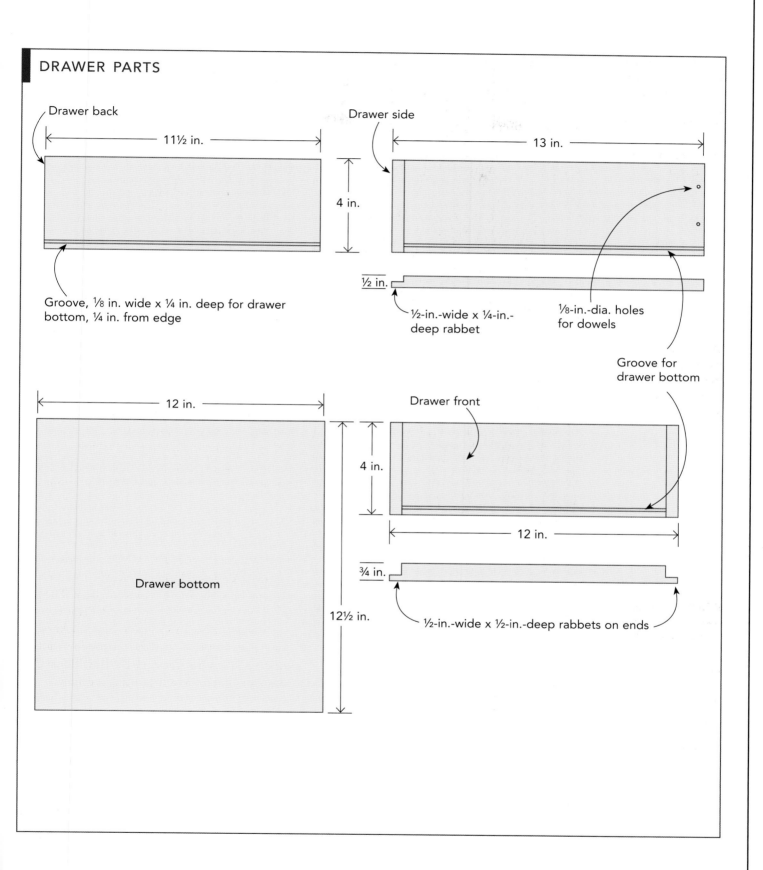

Drawer back

11½ in.

Drawer side

13 in.

4 in.

½ in.

Groove, ⅛ in. wide x ¼ in. deep for drawer bottom, ¼ in. from edge

½-in.-wide x ¼-in.-deep rabbet

⅛-in.-dia. holes for dowels

Groove for drawer bottom

12 in.

Drawer bottom

12½ in.

Drawer front

4 in.

12 in.

¾ in.

½-in.-wide x ½-in.-deep rabbets on ends

RABBET THE DRAWER FRONT. Use a dado set in the tablesaw to cut rabbets in the drawer front, which will house the drawer sides.

ADD A GROOVE FOR THE BOTTOM. Groove the drawer parts to hold the drawer bottom.

When cutting short pieces like these drawer parts, always use a push pad to keep your hands safely away from the sawblade.

FOURTH TEST. Once you have milled the major parts for the drawer, check their fit.

drawer front. Make the rabbets ½ in. wide and ½ in. deep. Then cut a rabbet in each drawer side to house the drawer back. You may need to change the blade height and stack width to accomplish this. Follow the plan on p. 75 for the location of the rabbets.

Change the dado set to a regular sawblade (not a thin-kerf blade) and cut the drawer back to length. It should be ½ in. shorter than the drawer front. Finally, cut the plywood for the bottom to size. Cut a groove in the front, back, and sides for the bottom panel, as shown on the plan. Make the groove ¼ in. deep.

Use a clamp to hold the drawer back and sides together. Slide the drawer bottom into place. Fit the front in place, capturing the bottom panel in the groove.

GLUE UP AND FINE-TUNE THE FIT

Check the dry-fit drawer for square. If everything looks right, proceed to glue the sides and back in place. Don't glue in the bottom panel. The drawer body must be flat and square for it to slide smoothly. To check for flatness, I place the drawer on the tablesaw, the flattest surface in the shop. If the drawer wobbles, I sand or plane down the high spot. Fortunately, the rabbet joinery I use for this drawer helps ensure that it comes out flat.

Once the glue has cured, check the fit in the opening. If the drawer seems too tight against the runners, plane the sides until it slides freely. Position the drawer so the front is flush with the front of the drawer support and the front top rail. Lightly clamp the drawer in place and glue stop blocks to the rear support, to prevent the drawer from sliding too far into the opening.

ADD PINS TO THE RABBETS

Reinforce the front joints with two $\frac{1}{8}$-in. dowels or pins. Drill a pair of $\frac{1}{8}$-in. holes through the side pieces and into the drawer front. Cut short lengths of dowel (a contrasting wood like walnut or even ebony will look great here). Apply glue to the dowels and tap them into the holes. Once the glue has cured, use a chisel and sandpaper to make the dowels flush with the drawer sides.

Finishing Touches

I like to use no-mortise hinges on the nightstand door. This type of hinge gives the look of a classic barrel hinge without the fuss of mortising the leaves into the case and door.

Attach the hinges to the door so the ends align with the top and bottom rails. Mark the location of the screw holes, drill pilot holes, and screw the hinges into place. Position the door in the opening and hold it in place with wedges or shims. Use an X-ACTO® knife to transfer the

FIT THE DRAWER. Position the drawer so it's flush with the front of the case and glue in blocks at the rear to prevent it from sliding in too far.

BRING IN REINFORCEMENTS. Drill holes in the drawer sides, then glue and tap in dowels to reinforce the rabbet joints. It's nice to use contrasting wood—lighter, as here, or darker.

hinge leaf location to the door frame. Pull the door out of the case, align the hinge leaf with the mark on the door, and mark the location of the screw holes. Drill pilot holes, then screw the hinges in place on the door.

I use a bullet catch to keep the door closed. Drill a hole into the edge of the door (instructions with the ball catch will tell you what size drill to use) and seat the ball portion of the catch. Close the door and transfer the location of the ball to the carcase. Drill a hole for the catch portion.

EASY HINGES. You can install no-mortise hinges quickly. Begin by screwing the hinges to the door frame. Then attach them to the case.

INSTALL A DOOR CATCH. Drill a hole in the door frame to hold the bullet catch, and a similar hole in the case to hold the strike for the catch.

To help ensure that you won't push the door in too far, glue a small stop block to the back side of the lower drawer support. This gives the door something to close against. Finish the door by attaching the pull.

Wrap up construction by attaching the top to the carcase with figure-8 fasteners. Use a Forstner bit to drill a shallow 7/8-in.-dia. recess in the top of the upper side rail (see p. 65). Position the point on the drill bit about 1/16 in. from the inner edge of the rail; don't center the bit on the rail. Screw one side of the figure-8 fastener into the recess. Slide the top into position on the case. Screw the other side of the figure 8 onto the top. Now, all you have to do to finish the nightstand is to install the drawer pull.

ADD HARDWARE. Measure for and drill mounting holes for the pulls on the drawer and the door.

FINISH AT THE TOP. Screw the top in place, using figure-8 connecters that are attached in recesses in the top rails.

7 WRITING DESK IN THE GREENE & GREENE STYLE

The architects Charles and Henry Greene had an enormous impact on the Arts & Crafts movement in the western U.S. At the turn of the 20th century, the brothers set up their practice in Pasadena, Calif., and over the next three decades created several distinctive bungalows. The Greenes did not merely design the structures; like Frank Lloyd Wright in the Midwest, they also designed the furniture and decorative objects.

Several features make Greene & Greene furniture unique. The stretchers on desks, tables, and breakfronts curve at the ends to form a "cloud lift" shape. Square pegs made of dark wood reinforce joints and add a decorative element. The brothers also used dark wood for splines to reinforce certain joints, and the ends of the splines are on full view. Board edges are softened, or slightly rounded over. The Greenes also tended to favor box joints over dovetails for drawers and the like.

Although not an exact replica of a Greene & Greene design, the desk in this chapter features many of those design elements: a simple cloud lift on the stretchers, box joints on the drawers, softened edges, and a top with breadboard ends

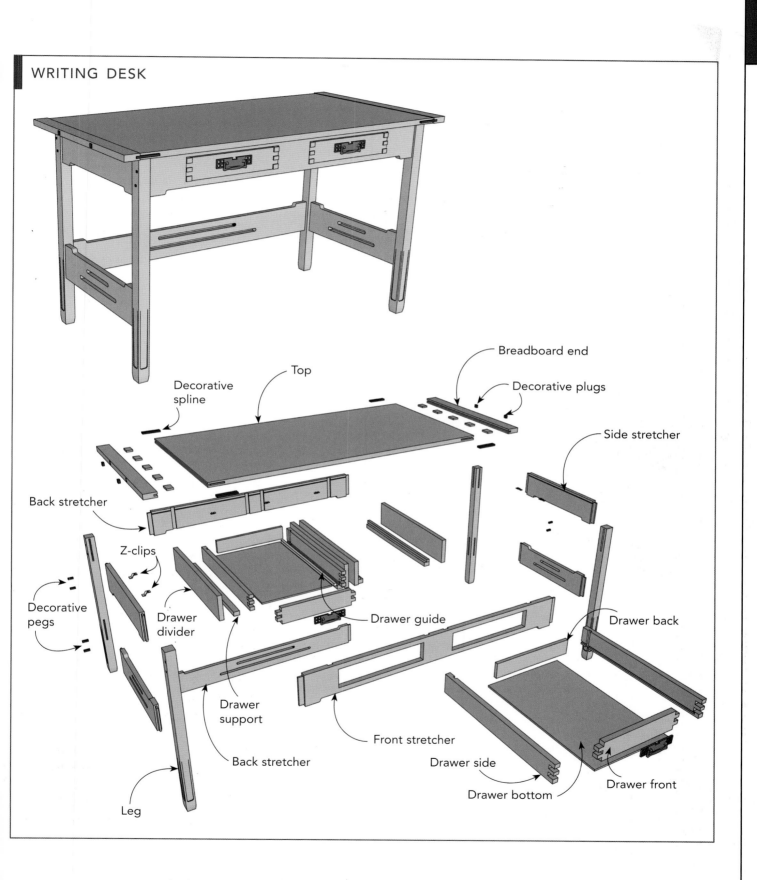

Breadboard end

Top

Decorative plugs

Decorative spline

Side stretcher

Back stretcher

Z-clips

Decorative pegs

Drawer divider

Drawer guide

Drawer back

Drawer support

Back stretcher

Front stretcher

Drawer side

Drawer front

Drawer bottom

Leg

that are reinforced with walnut splines. The desk is made of cherry, which is salmon-colored when freshly cut and turns a beautiful cinnamon brown as it ages.

Construction is very straightforward, with traditional mortise-and-tenon joints for the legs and stretchers. I'll show you how to create patterns and jigs for the router so you can make uniform cloud-lift shapes on all the stretchers and a striking tapered recess—another authentic Greene & Greene design element—on the legs.

MATERIALS

QUANTITY	PART	THICKNESS*	WIDTH*	LENGTH*	MATERIAL
4	Legs	1½	1½	29¼	Cherry
2	Back stretchers	¾	5	43½	Cherry
1	Front stretcher	¾	5	43½	Cherry
4	Side stretchers	¾	5	20½	Cherry
1	Top	¾	24	46	Cherry
2	Breadboard ends	13/16	2	24⅜	Cherry
2	Drawer fronts	¾	2⅞	13½	Cherry
4	Drawer sides	¾	2⅞	20⅞	Secondary wood
2	Drawer backs	½	2⅜	12½	Secondary wood
2	Drawer bottoms	¼	12½	20¼	Plywood
3	Drawer guides	½	½	20½	Secondary wood
4	Drawer supports	¾	1	20	Secondary wood
4	Drawer dividers	¾	4½	20½	Secondary wood
8	Decorative pegs	¼	¼	13/16	Walnut or ebony
4	Decorative plugs	5/16	½	½	Walnut or ebony
4	Decorative splines	¼	11/16	3	Walnut or ebony
10	Splines	¼	1	1½	Secondary wood

Total Board Feet: 17¾

HARDWARE

QUANTITY	PART	THICKNESS*	WIDTH*	LENGTH*	MATERIAL
2	Drawer pulls		1⅛	5⅛	
7	Table top fasteners		⅝	1⅝	

* Measurements are in inches.

Make the Legs First

You'll need straight-grained 8/4 stock for the legs (the rest of the desk uses 4/4 material, planed down to ¾-in. thickness). If you can't get good 8/4 cherry, glue together two pieces of 4/4 stock; it's the same technique used for the legs on the nightstand (see chapter 6). For a great grain match if you laminate the legs, cut a 3½-in.-wide board in half lengthwise and fold it in on itself. This will produce pleasing figure on at least three sides.

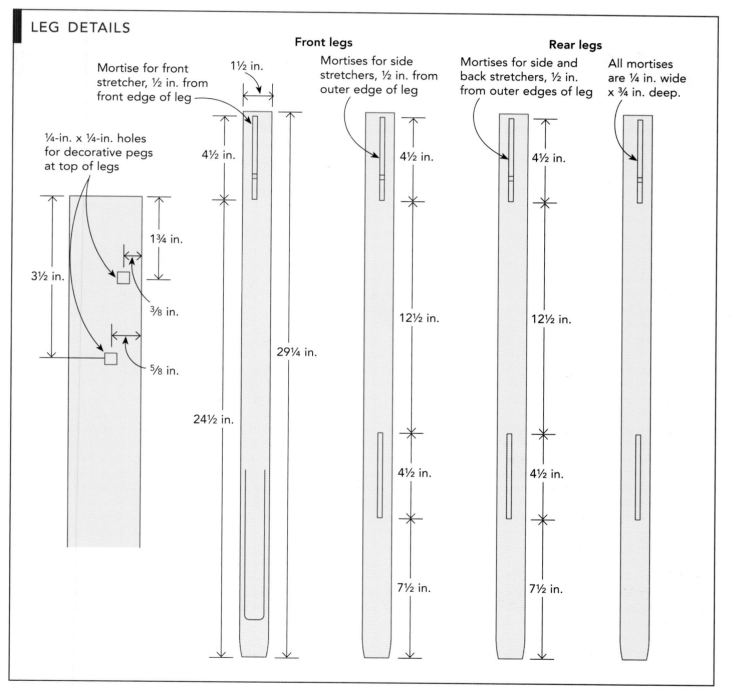

LEG DETAILS

Mortise for front stretcher, ½ in. from front edge of leg

¼-in. x ¼-in. holes for decorative pegs at top of legs

Front legs

Mortises for side stretchers, ½ in. from outer edge of leg

Rear legs

Mortises for side and back stretchers, ½ in. from outer edges of leg

All mortises are ¼ in. wide x ¾ in. deep.

1½ in.

3½ in.

1¾ in.

⅜ in.

⅝ in.

4½ in.

29¼ in.

24½ in.

4½ in.

12½ in.

4½ in.

7½ in.

4½ in.

12½ in.

4½ in.

7½ in.

THE BLACKER INDENT. A router and shopmade jig allow you to cut these tapered recesses in the legs quickly and uniformly. This photo also shows the curved taper at the end of the leg.

Jig for Making Tapered Recesses in Legs

Jigs are great time-savers, and they help make your woodworking accurate. Fortunately, jigs don't have to be expensive to make. The jig for the leg indent consists of four pieces of scrap, assembled to form a frame.

A fifth piece serves as a fence that's clamped to the workpiece. A shim under one end tilts the jig for the taper. If you make a similar jig but omit the shim, you can use it to cut the leg mortises.

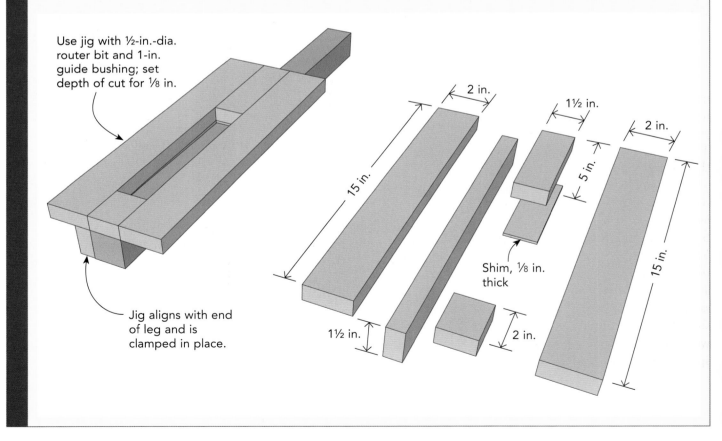

Use jig with ½-in.-dia. router bit and 1-in. guide bushing; set depth of cut for ⅛ in.

Jig aligns with end of leg and is clamped in place.

2 in.

1½ in.

2 in.

15 in.

5 in.

Shim, ⅛ in. thick

1½ in.

2 in.

15 in.

MILL AND MORTISE

After you have milled the legs to size following the cutlist on p. 82, arrange them so the best grain and figure are on the outside. Hold them together and mark the tops with a cabinet-maker's triangle to keep them oriented properly.

As you can see from the plan on p. 83, all the mortises in the legs are ¼ in. wide, 4½ in. long, and ¾ in. deep. Use your favorite method to cut them. I prefer to use a router with an edge guide and a spiral upcut bit.

ADD DECORATIVE ELEMENTS

At least two faces of each leg have a tapered recess near the bottom, which is commonly referred to as the Blacker indent, because this Greene & Greene motif first appeared on furniture made specifically for the Blacker House. (The sides that are mortised do not have a recess.) To make this distinctive shape, you'll need to build the jig shown on the facing page. It guides a router fitted with a ½-in.-dia. straight bit and a 1-in. guide bushing. A shim raises one end of the jig, so the router makes the tapered cut.

It's a good idea to practice on some scrap, mainly to establish the correct depth of cut. The recess is only ⅛ in. deep at the base. Once you've set the depth, begin cutting the real legs. The front legs have the indent on three faces; the rear legs, on two.

When you've finished cutting the tapered recesses, add a curved taper to the bottom of the legs. As the plan on p. 86 shows, the taper begins 1 in. up from the end of the leg and rolls ⅛ in. toward the center. Copy the pattern and use it to mark the faces of each leg so the curves are consistent. If you have an oscillating spindle sander or a disc sander, you can use them to shape the taper directly. Otherwise, saw a small wedge off each face of the leg and use a plane or spokeshave to create a fair curve.

TILTED JIG. This router jig has a shim at one end (see the drawing on the facing page), allowing you to cut a tapered recess in the legs.

FINISHED RECESS. Move the router around in the slot in the jig to cut the recess in one pass. Keep the router moving to avoid leaving burn marks in the wood.

Any edge that your fingers will touch should be rounded over. Use a ⅛-in. roundover bit in the router (or set up a router table for these cuts). Make them as you mill the boards to their final dimensions.

PATTERNS FOR LEG DETAILS AND CLOUD-LIFT SHAPE

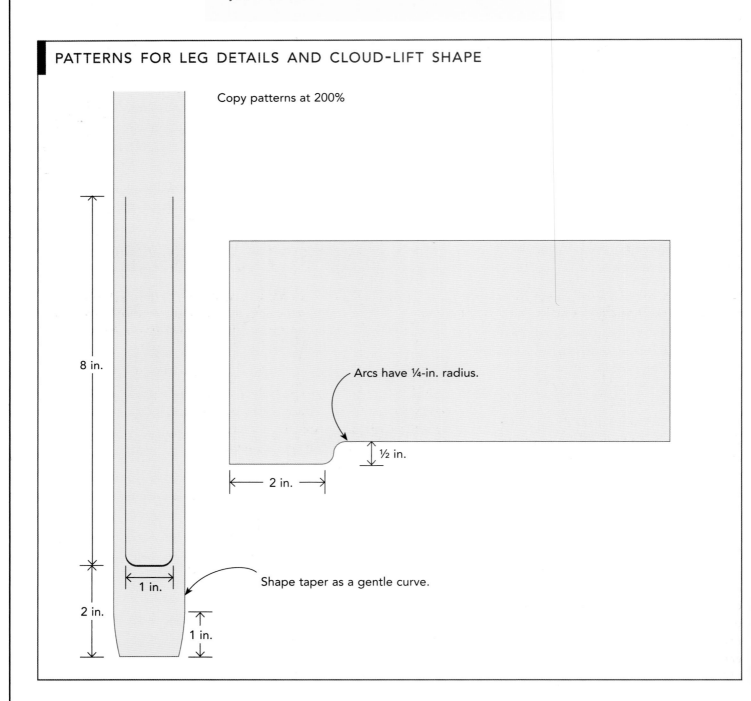

Copy patterns at 200%

Arcs have ¼-in. radius.

½ in.

2 in.

Shape taper as a gentle curve.

8 in.

1 in.

2 in.

1 in.

MEASURE CAREFULLY. Mark the centerline on the front stretcher and use it to make all other measurements for that part of the desk.

MARK FOR ALIGNMENT. Use chalk to put a carpenter's triangle over the centerline so you can keep parts oriented correctly later.

Cut the Stretchers and Drawer Fronts

For the most part, shaping the stretchers for the desk is pretty straightforward. Even with the cloud-lift detail, they are just long boards with a tenon on each end. The front stretcher, with the openings for the drawers, is another story. It requires care to shape accurately.

CHOP UP THE FRONT STRETCHER

The front stretcher is the most complicated part of the desk, so begin there. You'll make a series of rip cuts and crosscuts to get the drawer fronts out of the front stretcher. When the stretcher is reassembled and the drawers put in place, the grain will seem to be continuous across the face of the desk.

Begin by milling the front stretcher $1/16$ in. to $1/8$ in. thicker than its final thickness, and leave it extra-long and extra-wide for now. Measure along the length of the stretcher to find and mark its center. Make all other measurements from this centerline. Put a carpenter's triangle on the face of the board.

Following the plan on p. 88, rip the stretcher into three pieces. Set the narrow edge pieces aside and work on the wider center section. Mark the 5-in.-wide portion of the center section, measuring from the centerline toward each end. Cut out that section, using a crosscut sled on the tablesaw; be sure that the blade cuts to the waste side of each line. These cuts make the center portion. Mark the length of the drawer fronts on each end piece. Cut them out on the tablesaw and put them in a safe place. Set up a

STRETCHER DETAILS

Front stretcher

Stretcher is milled oversize in width and length and then ripped into three pieces; three spacers and two drawer fronts are cut from center section. Pieces are glued together; joinery and cloud-lift shapes are milled after glue-up.

Side stretchers

Saw kerf, ¼ in. deep, ⁷⁄₁₆ in. from top of upper side stretchers

Tenon, ¼ in. wide, centered on stretchers

Slots in lower side stretchers are same width and have same spacing as slots in lower back stretcher.

Upper back stretcher

Dadoes, ¾ in. wide × ¼ in. deep

Saw kerf, ¼ in. deep, ⁷⁄₁₆ in. from top of stretcher, for Z-clips that hold top in place (omit kerf on lower back stretcher)

Lower back stretcher

Slots, ½ in. wide, centered along length of stretcher

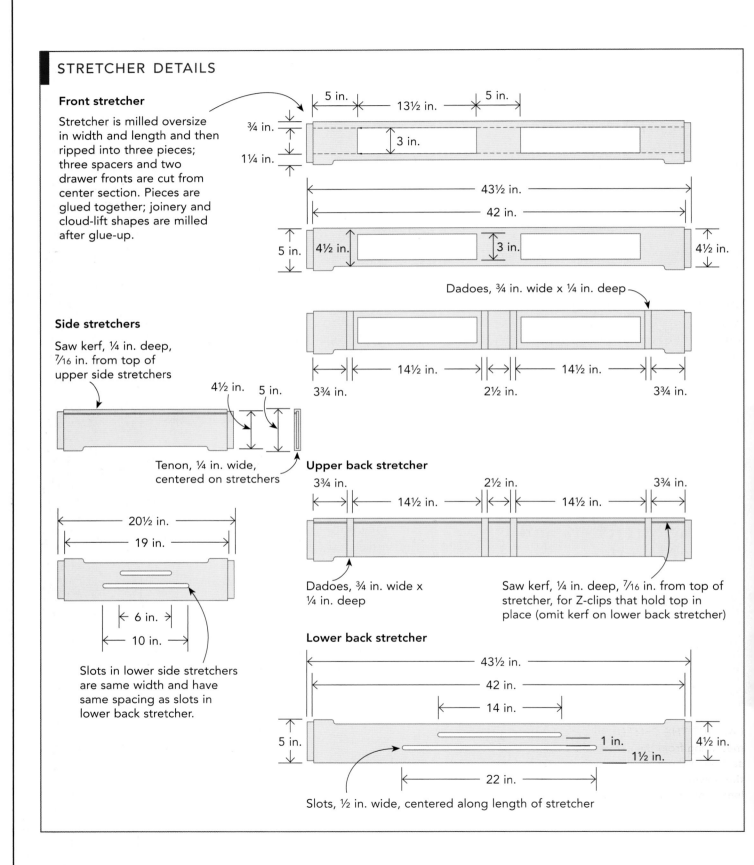

stop block on the crosscut sled so both fronts are identical, and again be sure the blade cuts on the waste side of the line. Finally, cut the two end pieces.

GLUE IT BACK TOGETHER

Reassemble the front stretcher. Align the center section with the edge pieces along the center-line. Use the drawer fronts as spacers to mark the position of the end pieces. Set the drawer fronts aside again and align the end pieces with those marks. Glue everything together, using plenty of clamps. Adjust the clamping pressure to ensure that all the pieces remain in the same plane. Placing clamps over the ends of the joints will help keep things in plane. Let the front stretcher cure overnight, then scrape off any excess glue squeeze-out.

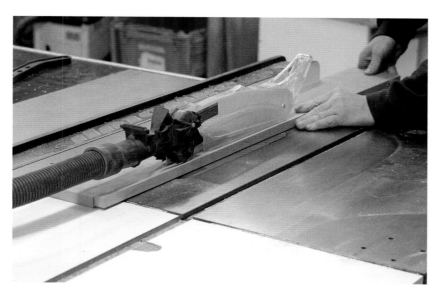

RIP THE STRETCHER. Follow measurements on the plan on the facing page to rip two narrow pieces off the top and bottom of the front stretcher.

CUT CAREFULLY. Use a crosscut sled, and be sure each cut in the front stretcher is on the waste side of the line.

LAY OUT THE CENTER PIECES. Following the plan and measuring from the center, mark the ends of the center section of the front rail. Cut it out, then measure the length of the drawer fronts and cut them. Finish by measuring the length of the end pieces and cutting them.

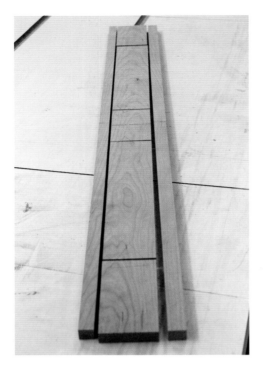

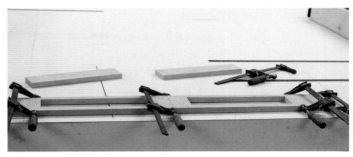

TOGETHER AGAIN. The front stretcher should look something like this when all the parts are cut and reassembled. On the finished desk, the grain will appear almost continuous across the stretcher.

CAREFUL GLUE-UP. Glue all the parts for the upper stretcher back together. Use the drawer fronts as place-holders (unglued, of course), to get the end pieces in the proper position.

TRIM THE STRETCHERS. Use a crosscut sled and stop blocks to trim all the stretchers to length. For the front stretcher, measure the length from the centerline toward each end.

CUT DECORATIVE SLOTS. Use a router with an edge guide to cut the two slots in the lower back stretcher. Cut a little more than half-way through on one face, then flip the board and finish the cut on the opposite face. This protects your bench and eliminates tearout.

Complete the Stretchers

Joint all the pieces for the long back stretchers and the side stretchers. When planing the stretchers to their final thickness, be sure to include the front stretcher, so it will be the exact same thickness as the others.

Square one end of each stretcher, using a crosscut sled on the tablesaw. Cut anywhere near one end of the side and back stretchers. For the front stretcher, though, measure half the finished length from the centerline toward one end to locate the position of the first cut. This is critical to ensure that the drawer openings are centered on the stretcher. Cut each stretcher to its final length, using stop blocks so that all the short and long stretchers are identical.

CUT SLOTS IN THE BACK STRETCHER

Using measurements from the plan on p. 88, mark the position of the two slots in the lower back stretcher. Mark both faces of the board. Make the slots with a plunge router fitted with an edge guide and a ½-in.-dia. spiral upcut bit. Set the depth of cut a hair deeper than ⅜ in. Set the edge guide so the bit aligns with one slot. Position the router at one end of the slot and plunge the bit into the wood. Cut to the opposite end of the slot in one pass. Flip the board over and repeat the cut on that face. This will prevent tearout in the stretcher and keep your workbench from being gouged by the router bit. Reset the edge guide and follow the same procedure to cut the second slot.

MAKE THE TENONS

All the stretchers have tenons that are ¼ in. thick and 4½ in. wide, with a ¼-in. shoulder on all four sides. You can cut them by hand or at the tablesaw, whichever you prefer. Check each tenon for fit, planing it as needed.

CUT DADOES IN THE STRETCHERS

The front and upper back stretchers have dadoes that house dividers for the drawers. Their position is critical, so that drawer supports and drawer guides fall in the proper place and are parallel.

Lay out guidelines for the four dadoes on both stretchers at once. Place them on a bench so their top edges butt and their inside faces point toward the ceiling. Align the ends and lightly clamp them together. Work from the centerline on the top stretcher and mark the position of each dado. Cut the dadoes on the tablesaw, using a dado set. Set up stop blocks for these cuts, to ensure that the dadoes align properly.

Design Inspirations

Asian design influenced the Greene brothers. The cloud-lift shapes they often used on their furniture mimic the stylized clouds seen in Chinese art.

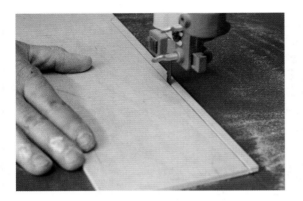

CLOUD-LIFT PATTERN. Trace or duplicate the pattern for the cloud-lift shape onto thin stock, following the plan on p. 86. Then carefully cut out the shape on the bandsaw and sand the edges smooth and even.

CUT THE CLOUD LIFTS

Make a pattern from a piece of ¼-in. plywood, or medium-density fiberboard (MDF), following the plan on p. 86. The pattern should be just a little longer than half the length of a back stretcher. Cut out the pattern, using a bandsaw or a jigsaw; smooth all the curves and plane the straight edges straight.

Transfer the cloud-lift shape onto all the stretchers and cut away the bulk of the waste with a bandsaw. Don't cut right to the pattern

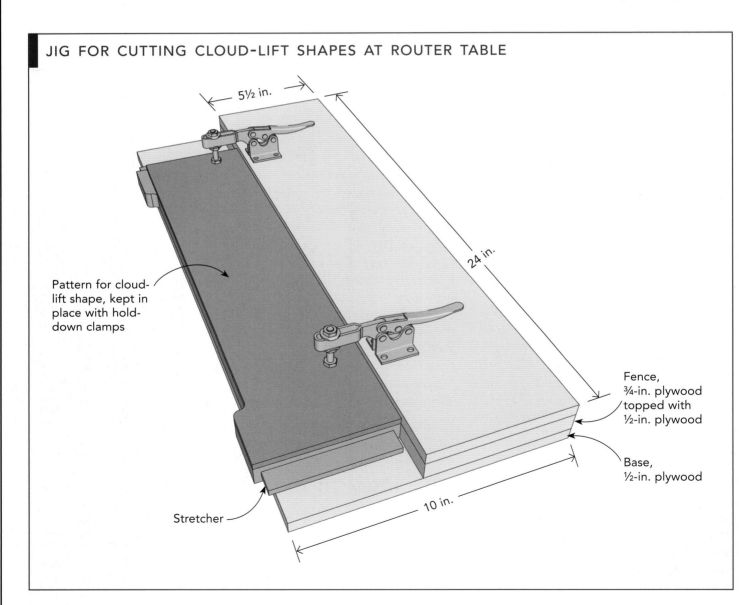

JIG FOR CUTTING CLOUD-LIFT SHAPES AT ROUTER TABLE

5½ in.

24 in.

Pattern for cloud-lift shape, kept in place with hold-down clamps

Fence, ¾-in. plywood topped with ½-in. plywood

Base, ½-in. plywood

Stretcher

10 in.

line, though. Leave ¹⁄₁₆ in. to ¹⁄₈ in. of material to be removed at the router table.

Orient a stretcher so its top edge faces you and the outside face points toward the ceiling. Attach the pattern to the left edge of the stretcher with double-sided tape; or make the pattern-holding jig shown on the facing page. Either way, be sure the pattern lines up with the top edge and the side of the stretcher. Outfit the router with a flush-trim bit that has a bottom-mounted bearing. Set the bit height so the bearing rides on the pattern and the cutter is just a touch higher than the thickness of the workpiece (see the photo at right).

Cut the cloud-lift profile on the stretcher, cutting just beyond the halfway point. Be sure to feed the pattern from right to left in order to avoid a climb cut. Remove the pattern and the double-stick tape. Flip the stretcher end for end and reattach the pattern. Rout only half the stretcher at a time to ensure that the router cuts downhill, or with the grain. If the router were to cut into the curves of the cloud-lift detail, it would likely catch the grain and cause major tearout. Repeat the procedure for all the remaining stretchers.

ADD A SAW KERF

At the tablesaw, make a ⁵⁄₁₆-in.-deep saw cut ⁷⁄₁₆ in. from the top edge of the inside face of the top side and rear stretchers (see the plan on p. 88). This will house the Z-shaped clips that hold the top in place.

Dry Fit and Get Ready for the Drawers

Connect the short stretchers to their legs and lightly clamp those assemblies together. Then (perhaps with the help of a friend), fit the long stretchers into their mortises and clamp everything together. Be sure the four top stretchers are flush with the tops of the legs. If a component needs to be positioned higher or lower, trim the short shoulder of the tenon so you can

adjust the stretcher at glue-up. Likewise, measure to be sure the top edges of the bottom stretchers are at a consistent height; trim the tenons if need be.

Use a secondary wood like poplar to make the drawer dividers, supports, and guides, following the measurements in the cutlist. Mill the

SHAPE THE CLOUD LIFTS. Secure the pattern to a stretcher, then use a router with a bottom-mounted bearing to trim the stretcher so it matches the pattern. The bearing should ride just above the stretcher.

ASSEMBLE THE FRAME. Dry-fit the legs and stretchers to check the joinery and prepare the interior stretchers and runners for the drawers.

Although the plans
give a length for the
internal stretchers, it's
more accurate to
measure the length
directly from the dry-
fit desk.

wood for these pieces to their final width and
thickness, but leave them long.

The cutlist gives a length for the dividers, but
it's the ideal length. For accuracy, take the measurement directly from the desk itself. Measure
from the bottom of a dado on the back stretcher
to the bottom of the corresponding dado on the
front. Cut the dividers to size using a crosscut
sled on the tablesaw; clamp a stop block to the
sled so the pieces will be identical. Add the
dividers to the dry-fit desk.

Add the drawer supports. Take the length
directly from the desk itself. Once you've cut
them to length, glue them to the dividers. Do
the same for the drawer guides. Before gluing
them to the supports, be sure they do not project past the openings for the drawers in the
front stretcher. If one guide does, plane it down
as needed.

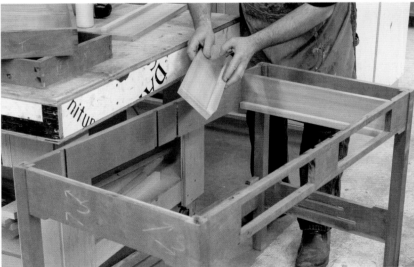

ADD STRETCHERS AND SUPPORTS. Attach the drawer guides to the
stretchers, then fit the assembly into the dadoes in the front and back
top stretchers.

Make the Drawers

Begin by milling the pieces for the sides and back to their final width and thickness. Cut the sides to length, but leave the back pieces long for now.

CUT THE BOX JOINTS

Taking the measurements from the plan below, carefully lay out the box joints on the front and side pieces. Mark a large X in each waste area, so you don't inadvertently cut away the wrong part. The joints on the sides are $\frac{7}{8}$ in. deep, while those on the fronts are $\frac{3}{4}$ in. deep. It's part of the Greene & Greene style to have part of a joint like this stand proud of its mate.

To cut the joints, screw a tall auxiliary fence to the tablesaw's miter gauge and install a ripping blade with a flat raker tooth. You can cut the box joints in the sides or the front first; the sequence doesn't matter. The process is the same

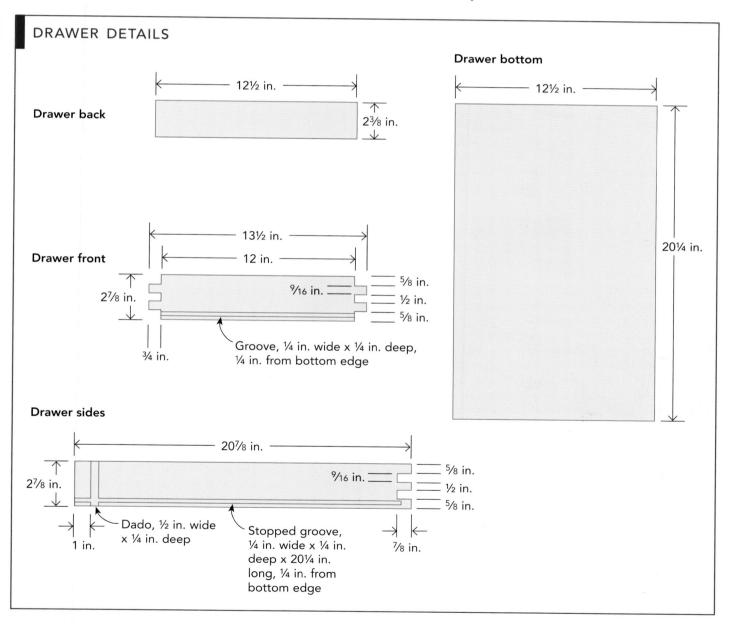

DRAWER DETAILS

Drawer back — 12½ in., 2⅜ in.

Drawer bottom — 12½ in., 20¼ in.

Drawer front — 13½ in., 12 in., 2⅞ in., ¾ in., 9/16 in., ⅝ in., ½ in., ⅝ in.
Groove, ¼ in. wide x ¼ in. deep, ¼ in. from bottom edge

Drawer sides — 20⅞ in., 2⅞ in., 1 in., 9/16 in., ⅝ in., ½ in., ⅝ in., ⅞ in.
Dado, ½ in. wide x ¼ in. deep
Stopped groove, ¼ in. wide x ¼ in. deep x 20¼ in. long, ¼ in. from bottom edge

LAY OUT THE BOX JOINTS. Lay out the joints on the drawer fronts and drawer sides. Be sure to mark an X in the spaces to be cut away.

FIRST CUT. Align the tablesaw blade with one layout line. Clamp a stop block on the fence so you can make identical cuts in the other parts.

SECOND CUT. Align the blade with the next layout line. Clamp a second stop block on the fence. Now you can nibble away the waste in successive cuts.

WORK SMART

Using a blade with a flat raker tooth will ensure that the base of each cutout for the box joint is flat and square. A blade with alternating top-bevel teeth would leave a rougher surface that requires cleanup.

for each notch you have to cut: Align the blade to one layout line, making sure the blade is on the waste side of the line. Set a stop block on the fence. Then shift the workpiece so the blade aligns with the second layout line; again, be sure the blade is on the waste side of the line. Set another stop block. Adjust the blade height.

Hold the workpiece against one stop block, make the cut, then shift the workpiece to the second stop block and make the second cut. Now just make repeated cuts, nibbling away the waste. Cut the same notch in both drawer fronts or all four side pieces before shifting the stop blocks for the next notch.

MAKE GROOVES AND DADOES

Cut a ¼-in. groove in the sides and front to house the drawer bottom. Use a router with an edge guide and ¼-in.-dia. spiral upcut bit. As the plan on p. 95 shows, the groove in the sides is stopped; that is, it doesn't run the full length of the piece. But it runs from edge to edge on the drawer front. To finish shaping the drawers, cut dadoes in the side pieces to house the back, using a dado set in the tablesaw.

FINE-TUNE THE FIT

If the joints are tight, carefully pare away wood with a chisel until you get a fit that's slightly snug. If the joints are loose, pare a very thin piece of cherry from a piece of scrap and use it as a shim.

CUT THE BACK AND BOTTOM, AND GLUE UP

Cut the drawer bottoms from ¼-in. plywood. Dry-fit the drawers and measure between dadoes to determine the length of the back pieces. Cut the backs to size and slide them in place. When everything looks right and is square, glue up the drawers and let them cure overnight.

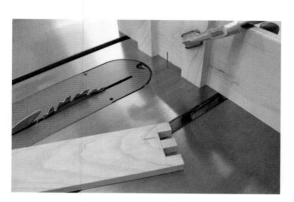

FINAL CUTS. Once you have cut one space away, flip the workpiece over so you can cut the other space.

A SLOT FOR THE DRAWER BOTTOM. Use a router with an edge guide to cut a slot in the drawer front and sides to house the drawer bottom.

TEST FIT. Dry-fit the drawer parts to be sure the finger joints are suitably tight. The fingers on the drawer sides will be about ⅛-in. proud of the drawer front.

Fabricate the Top

Begin by milling the boards for the main section of the top to their final width and ¾-in. thickness. Arrange them for the best grain match and glue up the panel (see chapter 3). Next day, when the glue has cured, scrape off any squeeze-out and rip the panel to its final width and length. Mill the boards for the breadboard ends to their final width and ¹³⁄₁₆-in. thickness. The fatter ends on tabletops are another hallmark of Greene & Greene style.

CUT GROOVES, GLUE IN SPLINES

Use a router fitted with a ¼-in.-dia. spiral upcut bit and an edge guide to cut a groove for the splines on each end of the main panel. Reference the edge guide on the bottom face of the panel. Without changing the router setting, cut another groove on one edge of the breadboard end pieces; again, reference the edge guide on the bottom face of the boards.

Find a piece of secondary wood that's 3 in. to 4 in. wide. Plane it to ¼-in. thickness so it fits snugly in the table-panel grooves. Cut at least ten splines, each 1½ in. long, from this piece. Fit the splines into the groove in the main panel. Put one spline in the center and space

WORK SMART

When you use a router to cut a groove on the edge of a board, gang multiple pieces together or clamp some extra pieces of scrap to the faces of the board. This adds stability and helps prevent the router from wobbling.

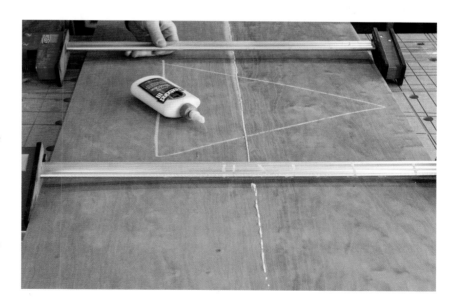

GLUE UP THE TOP. Assemble the center section of the top from ¾-in.-thick material. Two wide pieces, as shown here, are ideal, but three or more narrower pieces can also work well.

ATTACHING THE BREADBOARD ENDS

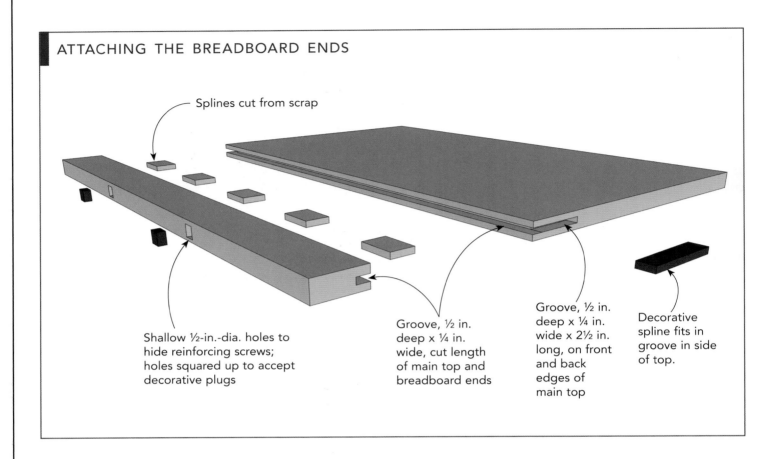

Splines cut from scrap

Shallow ½-in.-dia. holes to hide reinforcing screws; holes squared up to accept decorative plugs

Groove, ½ in. deep x ¼ in. wide, cut length of main top and breadboard ends

Groove, ½ in. deep x ¼ in. wide x 2½ in. long, on front and back edges of main top

Decorative spline fits in groove in side of top.

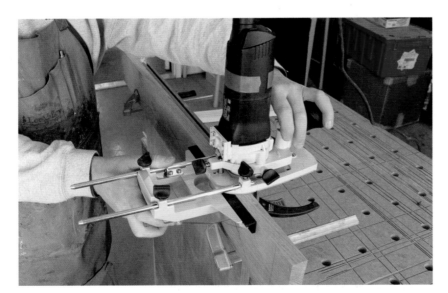

GROOVE THE ENDS OF THE TOP. Use a router to cut a groove on each end of the top. Clamp one or two boards to the side of the top, to help support the router and prevent it from tipping as you make the cut.

the others evenly along the width. Keep the splines at least 1 in. from the edges of the panel.

Next day, when the glue has dried, attach the breadboard ends. This time, apply glue only to the center spline; the others need to be free to move as the top expands and contracts with changes in humidity. Slide the breadboard ends in place. Position them so they extend past the center panel by about ⅛ in. front and back. Tighten the clamps.

REINFORCE THE JOINT

Drive two long screws through each breadboard end to reinforce the splined joint. Bore a hole ¼ in. to ⅜ in. deep with a ½-in. Forstner bit. Then drill a smaller pilot hole for the screw in the center of this hole. Wobble the bit as you drill into the breadboard end to enlarge the hole slightly to allow for seasonal wood movement.

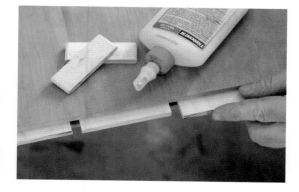

INSERT SPLINES. Space four or five splines in each groove in the top, keeping them at least 1 in. from the ends.

EXTRA HOLD. After attaching the breadboard end with short splines, reinforce the joint with two long screws driven through the end of the breadboard. Cap the holes with a decorative peg.

SIMPLE SPACER. Use a washer as a spacer to draw the line showing how far this decorative spline extends past the end of the desk top.

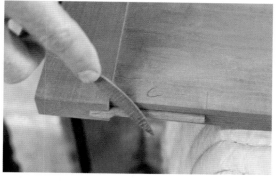

FILE TO THE LINE. Shape the spline by sawing close to the guideline, then finishing with a small rasp or file. Round over all the edges for an authentic Greene & Greene look.

Use a chisel to square up each of the large, shallow holes. After you've driven the screws, cut square walnut pegs to fill the holes and glue them in place.

ADD DECORATIVE SPLINES

Pick up the router you used to cut the grooves for the structural splines. Set its depth of cut to ½ in. and cut grooves on the edges of the top, which extend a total of 2½ in. from the top/breadboard end seam. Square up the ends with a chisel.

Cut pieces of walnut (or ebony, if you can afford it) to be the same thickness as the grooves on the edges and as long as the grooves are wide. Glue these decorative splines into their grooves, but apply glue only on the main-panel side of the groove so that the piece can move with seasonal changes in humidity. These splines will be slightly proud of the tabletop. Hold a washer against the tabletop to serve as a spacer and run a pencil line across the spline. Saw off the excess spline at this line, then smooth and fair it with a block plane, chisels, and sandpaper.

SQUARE PEGS. After drilling the legs for decorative pegs, square up the holes. You can use a chisel or a square punch, as shown here.

Glue Up, Add Decorative Pegs and Hardware

Use the same sequence you did for the dry-fit to do the glue-up: Glue the ends together, checking for square. Then glue in the long stretchers, again checking for square. When the glue has cured for a couple of hours, invert the assembly onto the underside of the top. Measure to be sure the overhang is the same on each side and consistent along the front. Slide the Z-clips into the saw kerfs in the top stretchers and screw the clips to the top. Use two clips on each side, three on the back. Using this kind of hardware is a time-saving alternative to shopmade "buttons," small blocks of wood with a tongue on one end that fits in the groove in the stretcher.

Following the plan on p. 83, drill shallow holes for decorative pegs in the legs. Square up the holes with a chisel and fill them with pieces of walnut or ebony. (If you plan to use a lot of square pegs in your woodworking, you can invest in a square hole punch; it makes quick work of the task.) Trim the pegs slightly proud, using a washer for a spacer, as described above. Use a piece of sanding foam to round over the edges of the pegs.

The drawer hardware I prefer is a pull from Lee Valley® (item no. 01A28.40). However, you could make your own wood pulls from mahogany or ebony. The finish I prefer is my 321 mixture of oil, varnish, and solvent; see chapter 11 for the recipe.

WORK SMART

To cut all the pegs to a consistent height, I rest a flush trim saw against a shim of Masonite® (with a hole in the center), which acts as a spacer.

FINISHING TOUCH. Screw the pulls to the two drawer fronts.

GREENE & GREENE–INSPIRED SIDE CHAIR

This chair is the perfect complement to the desk constructed in the previous chapter. You can use the same router jigs and templates to shape the legs and add the cloud-lift detail to the stretchers and back slats. The chair goes together with straightforward mortise-and-tenon joinery, which has been used for all the previous projects in the book. The ends of the side stretchers are cut at a slight angle, which could make it difficult to join legs to stretchers. If you construct the chair with loose tenons, though, the angled shoulders won't be a problem.

The padded seat is fairly straightforward. Even so, it would probably be best to have a professional upholsterer handle this part of the project.

Mill the Legs First

Construct the chair legs just the way you did the desk legs: Either utilize 8/4 stock or make a lamination of two layers. The back legs are cut from a 6-in.-wide blank, so mill those boards accordingly. Joint and plane the front-leg blanks to their final width and thickness, and the back leg blank to 1½ in. thick and 6 in. wide.

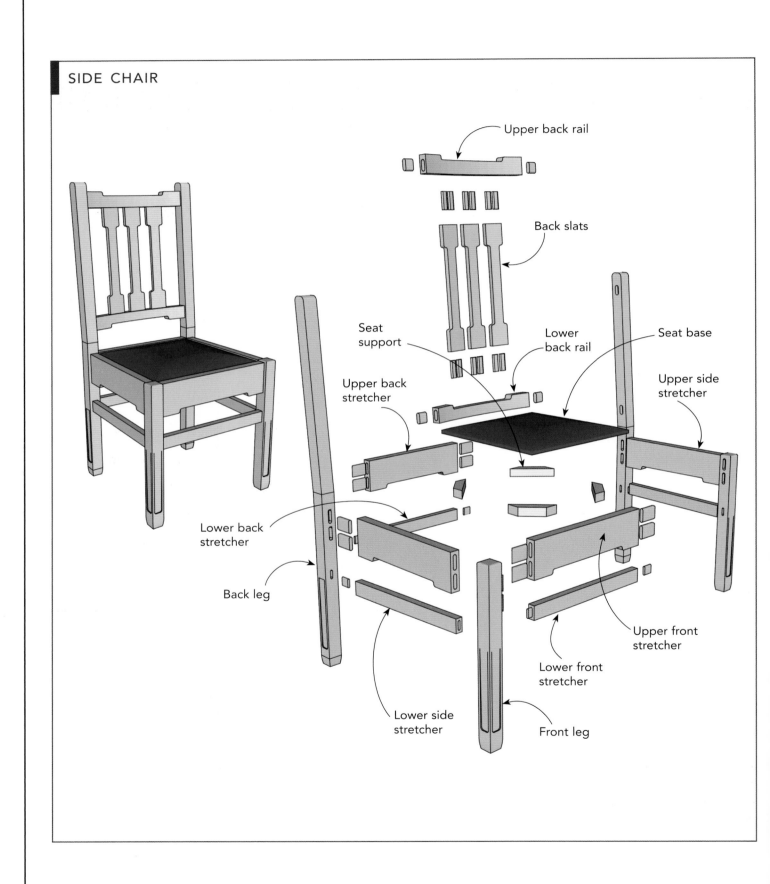

Upper back rail

Back slats

Seat support

Lower back rail

Seat base

Upper side stretcher

Upper back stretcher

Lower back stretcher

Back leg

Lower side stretcher

Front leg

Lower front stretcher

Upper front stretcher

MATERIALS

QUANTITY	PART	THICKNESS*	WIDTH*	LENGTH*	MATERIAL
2	Front legs	1½	1½	18³⁄₁₆	Cherry
2	Back legs	1½	6	40	Cherry
1	Upper front stretcher	1	4	15	Cherry
1	Upper back stretcher	1	4	14	Cherry
2	Upper side stretchers	1	4	14½	Cherry
1	Lower front stretcher	¾	1½	15	Cherry
1	Lower back stretcher	¾	1½	14	Cherry
2	Lower side stretchers	¾	1½	14½	Cherry
1	Upper back rail	1¾	2	14	Cherry
1	Lower back rail	1¾	1¾	14	Cherry
3	Back slats	½	2¼	14³⁄₁₆	Cherry
4	Seat supports	1	1	3⅝	Secondary wood
12	Back slat tenons	¼	1½	2	Secondary wood
8	Lower stretcher tenons	½	1	2	Secondary wood
16	Upper stretcher tenons	½	1½	2	Secondary wood
4	Back rail tenons	½	1¼	2	Secondary wood
1	Seat base	½	14½	15	Plywood

Total Board Feet: 9½

* Measurements are in inches.

SHAPE THE BACK LEGS

Following the measurements on the plan on p. 104, lay out the profile of the back legs on a piece of ¼-in. plywood or medium-density fiberboard. Cut out the pattern at the bandsaw, and sand the edges smooth and straight. Use the pattern with a bearing-guided router bit to shape the legs; it's the same procedure used to put the cloud-lift shapes on the stretchers for the desk (see p. 92).

CUT THE MORTISES

Use the plans on pp. 104 and 105 to lay out all the mortises on the leg blanks. Then use your favorite method to cut them. For this project, I'm using a Festool Domino, a handheld power tool that cuts mortises to fit special loose tenons. A router and spiral upcut bit will work equally well. Remember to register the edge guide against the same face on each leg. That is, if you cut the mortises on the first leg with the

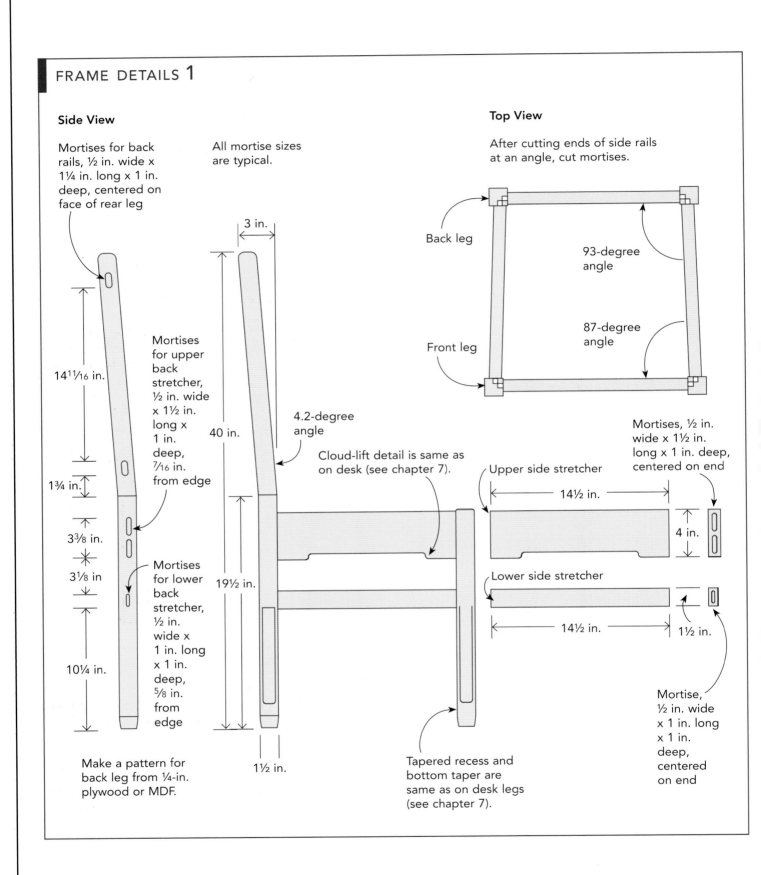

FRAME DETAILS 1

Side View

Mortises for back rails, ½ in. wide x 1¼ in. long x 1 in. deep, centered on face of rear leg

All mortise sizes are typical.

14¹¹⁄₁₆ in.

1¾ in.

Mortises for upper back stretcher, ½ in. wide x 1½ in. long x 1 in. deep, ⁷⁄₁₆ in. from edge

3⅜ in.

3⅛ in

Mortises for lower back stretcher, ½ in. wide x 1 in. long x 1 in. deep, ⅝ in. from edge

10¼ in.

Make a pattern for back leg from ¼-in. plywood or MDF.

3 in.

40 in.

4.2-degree angle

Cloud-lift detail is same as on desk (see chapter 7).

19½ in.

1½ in.

Tapered recess and bottom taper are same as on desk legs (see chapter 7).

Top View

After cutting ends of side rails at an angle, cut mortises.

Back leg

93-degree angle

87-degree angle

Front leg

Mortises, ½ in. wide x 1½ in. long x 1 in. deep, centered on end

Upper side stretcher

14½ in.

4 in.

Lower side stretcher

14½ in.

1½ in.

Mortise, ½ in. wide x 1 in. long x 1 in. deep, centered on end

FRAME DETAILS 2

Front View

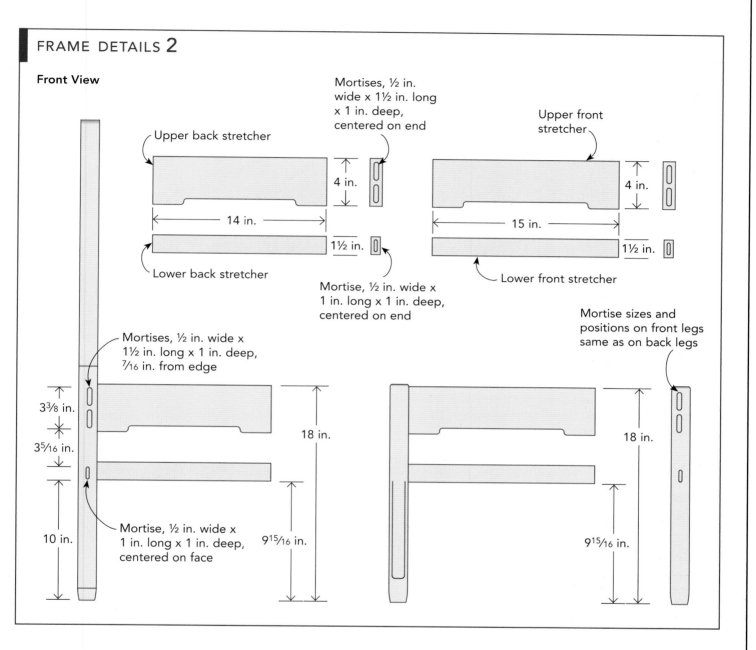

Mortises, ½ in. wide x 1½ in. long x 1 in. deep, centered on end

Upper back stretcher

Upper front stretcher

4 in.

4 in.

14 in.

15 in.

1½ in.

1½ in.

Lower back stretcher

Lower front stretcher

Mortise, ½ in. wide x 1 in. long x 1 in. deep, centered on end

Mortise sizes and positions on front legs same as on back legs

Mortises, ½ in. wide x 1½ in. long x 1 in. deep, 7/16 in. from edge

3⅜ in.

3⁵⁄₁₆ in.

18 in.

18 in.

10 in.

Mortise, ½ in. wide x 1 in. long x 1 in. deep, centered on face

9¹⁵⁄₁₆ in.

9¹⁵⁄₁₆ in.

fence on an outside face, then cut the mortises on all the other legs with the fence on the outside face.

Mill the Stretchers

These are the wide and narrow pieces that connect the legs below the seat. The initial shaping is completely straightforward. All the fancy parts are added later.

PREPARE THE STOCK

Mill the four wide and four narrow stretchers to their final width and thickness, following the measurements in the cutlist. Leave the side stretchers overlong for now, but cut the front and back stretchers to their final length. Look over the pieces and choose the best face on each stretcher for the outside face. Mark that face with chalk.

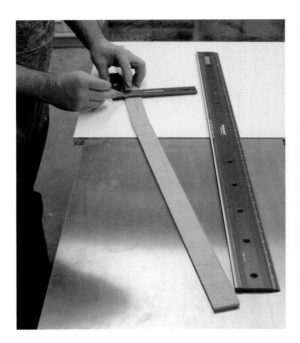

PATTERN TELLS A STORY. Make a pattern for the back leg from thin plywood or MDF. Use it as a story stick—a woodworker's tool that gives all important dimensions. Here, I'm laying out locations for the lower stretchers. Later, I'll transfer these measurements to the leg blanks.

TRACE THE SHAPE. Outline the pattern on the thick leg blanks. Using a pattern for parts like these chair legs helps ensure that they will be identical.

SAW CAREFULLY. At the bandsaw, rough out the back leg shape. Cut close to the line, always on the waste side.

CLEAN UP. Use brads or double-sided tape to attach the pattern to the leg. Then refine the shape at the router table, using a bearing-guided bit.

MORTISE THE LEGS. Begin the joinery with the legs. Here, I'm using a tool that cuts mortises sized to specific loose tenons. But you can just as easily use a router or drill press.

ANGLE THE SIDE STRETCHERS

Like most chairs, this one is wider at the front of the seat than at the back. The front and back stretchers are parallel, however, which means that the side stretchers must splay at a slight angle to connect front to back. You can see this clearly in the plan on p. 104. Begin by setting a bevel gauge for a 3-degree angle. Use it first to tilt the tablesaw blade. Then use the gauge to lay out the angle at one end of the four side stretchers.

Line up one stretcher so the blade will cut just to the waste side of the layout line. Clamp a stop block to the miter fence and make the cut. Make the same cut on all four stretchers. Measure the stretcher's length from one angled end and mark the corresponding angle at the opposite end. The angled layout lines should be parallel. Carry the lines around the other faces of the stretcher.

Flip the stretchers end for end, lining them up so the blade cuts just to the waste side of the

SET UP AN ANGLE. Put a 3-degree angle on a bevel gauge and use it to tilt the blade on the tablesaw so you can cut the ends of the side stretchers.

MARK ONE END. Without changing the angle on the miter gauge, use it to mark one edge of a side stretcher.

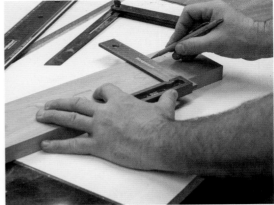

MARK THE LENGTH. Measure the length of the stretcher and mark it on the face of the board. Mark the angle and cut to length.

MAKE ONE CUT. Cut the side stretcher at the angle mark you just made. Be sure to cut just to the waste side of the line.

guideline at the other end of the stretcher. Make the cuts as before.

Lay out the location of the mortises in the ends of the stretchers and cut them as you did the mortises on the legs. The mortises must be cut square to the ends of the side stretchers.

SHAPE THE TENONS

Making the floating tenons uses the same procedure as that for the bed in chapter 5. You'll just be making smaller pieces this time. Even so, you'll need more than 6 ft. of stock to make all the tenons the chair requires. The stretchers alone use two dozen 2-in. tenons; the back

MORTISES NEXT. Cut mortises in the ends of the lower stretchers and the two back rails.

If you use a router to cut the mortises in the stretchers, make sure the router is well supported. Clamp scrap blocks to the stretchers so you can steady the router and prevent it from wobbling as it cuts on the narrow ends of the boards.

slats require a dozen tenons, and the back rails require four. You can use a secondary wood rather than cherry for the tenons. Mill the stock to ½-in. thickness (except for the back-slat tenons, which are ¼ in.), and test the fit in a leg mortise. Plane if necessary to achieve a snug fit. Then cut the tenons to width and length and round over the narrow faces so they fit the mortises.

Add the Back Components

Begin by milling the rails and back slats. The curved back rails will be cut from thick stock; mill those parts to width but leave them thick for now. Mill the slats to their final dimensions. Leave the rails and slats square for now. You'll shape the rails and add cloud lifts to the slats later.

Lay out the location of the mortises for the two back rails in the back leg (see the plan on p. 104). Cut them as you did the others.

BACK COMPONENTS

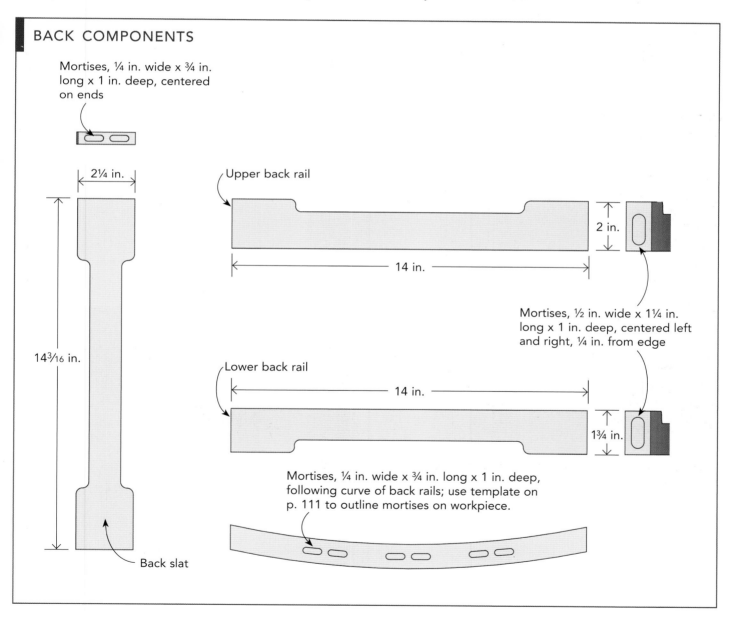

Mortises, ¼ in. wide x ¾ in. long x 1 in. deep, centered on ends

2¼ in.

14³⁄₁₆ in.

Back slat

Upper back rail

14 in.

2 in.

Mortises, ½ in. wide x 1¼ in. long x 1 in. deep, centered left and right, ¼ in. from edge

Lower back rail

14 in.

1¾ in.

Mortises, ¼ in. wide x ¾ in. long x 1 in. deep, following curve of back rails; use template on p. 111 to outline mortises on workpiece.

WORK
SMART

When making a fairly complex piece like this chair, plan ahead and devise a logical way to work so that the stock is always well supported. For the back rails, for instance, make the back-slat mortises first, then cut the cloud-lift shapes. Cut their curves last.

CUT MORTISES FOR THE BACK SLATS

To make sure the mortises for the back slats line up and the slats are in line, use the full-size pattern on the facing page. Trace the pattern onto a piece of paper or thin cardboard and cut it out. Align the right edge of the pattern with the center of the blank for the back rail. Outline the mortise shapes, then flip the pattern and finish the tracing. If you do everything correctly, the center slat will be straight on and the flanking slats at a slight angle. Set these pieces aside for now; you'll finish them later.

The ends of the slats get a pair of mortises for thin loose tenons (see the plan on p. 109). Cut those mortises now.

Do a Test Fit

With all the parts cut to size and mortised, dry-fit everything. The mortises for the upper and lower stretchers will intersect, so trim the tenons for the stretchers at a 45-degree angle. Check that the angles between legs and stretchers at each side of the front and back are identical, and that the front and back legs are parallel.

FINISH THE LAYOUT. Transfer locations for the back-rail mortises from the story stick pattern to the back legs, then finish laying them out.

TRICKY LAYOUT. The mortises for the back slats are centered on the back rails and fall along a curve. To make this part of the joinery easy, the plan includes a full-size template you can use to locate the mortises precisely.

OBJECT LESSON. The back rails show the importance of following a logical sequence for joinery. It's easiest to cut the mortises first, then the cloud-lift shapes, and the curves last.

PATTERN FOR MORTISES IN BACK RAILS

Use at 100%

Align this corner with the centerline of the workpiece and the back edge.

DRY RUN. Assemble the chair without glue to check the fit of all the joints. You want to get them right before adding any embellishments.

TRIM THE TENONS. Because the mortises in the legs intersect, you will have to miter one end of the tenons so they fit together properly.

Fine-tune the fit of the tenons until you're satisfied with the way the legs and stretchers go together.

Add the Decorative Details

Use the router jig shown on p. 84 to cut the tapered recesses on two outside faces of each leg. Use the same procedures covered on p. 85. With that done, carve or sand the curved taper at the base of each leg. Here, too, the procedure is the same as that used on the desk legs.

Use the template shown in chapter 7 (p. 86) to cut the cloud-lift shapes in the wide lower stretchers. The procedure is the same as that for the desk. Use the router template to cut the cloud-lift shapes in the back rails. Because these rails are still thick, you may need to cut part-way through from one side, flip the stock, and make the cut from the opposite side.

At the bandsaw, cut the curves for the two back rails, then smooth the curves with a spokeshave, a spindle sander, a block plane, or whatever. Do another dry-fit to be sure the stretchers fit snugly against the back legs; fine-tune the fit with handplanes as needed.

Use the router template again to cut the cloud-lift shapes on each side of the slats.

ADD THE DECORATIVE RECESS.
The legs have the same tapered recess as the legs on the desk shown in the previous chapter. Use a router jig (see p. 84) to cut those shapes.

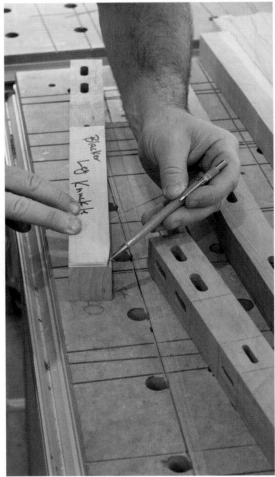

A CURVED TAPER.
The legs also have a curved taper to match the one on the desk legs. Here, I'm using a template to mark the curve. Plane or sand the shape on each leg.

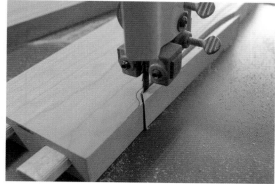

SAW AWAY WASTE. Begin shaping the cloud lifts at the bandsaw, cutting away most of the waste.

GATHERING CLOUDS. Lay out the cloud-lift shapes on the stretchers and the back rails. This is another instance where using a template speeds the work and ensures that all the pieces will be identical.

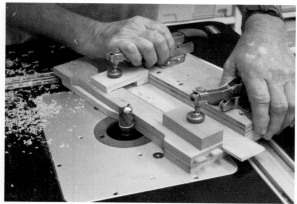

FINAL SHAPING. Use the cloud-lift pattern and a bearing-guided router bit to complete shaping the cloud lifts. The plan for the router jig is on p. 92.

CURVE THE SLATS. Rough out the back-rail curves at the bandsaw. Guide the blade on the waste side of the line for both cuts.

SAND RAILS SMOOTH. An oscillating belt sander makes quick work of fairing the curves on the back rails. A spindle sander or a spokeshave will also work.

FRONT LEGS FIRST. Begin the glue-up by assembling the front legs and stretchers.

BACK COMES NEXT. Fit the back slats into the back rails without glue, and use a clamp to hold those parts together, as shown here. Then glue the back legs in place.

Glue up the Chair

The glue-up is another instance where it's essential to plan ahead and come up with a logical, workable sequence for gluing together the parts. One reason you dry-fit a piece is to rehearse the sequence you'll follow when the glue actually goes in the joints. Glue the front stretchers into the front legs. Check to be sure the legs are parallel and the assembly is square. Do the same with the back stretchers in the back legs, adding the back rails and back slats as well. There's no need to glue the back slats into the rails, though. The slats add no strength to the chair; the tenons alone are enough to hold them in place. In addition, gluing slats just complicates the overall glue-up.

When those two assemblies have dried, glue the side stretchers in place, beginning with the joints in the back legs. Apply clamps to the front and back stretchers to pull the assembly together. Be sure everything is square and that the chair hasn't racked. Check how it rests on a dead flat surface, such as the top of your tablesaw or workbench. If it wobbles, check that the stretchers are even with the tops of the legs and adjust the clamps to make sure they are not pulling the chair out of square.

Cut the four seat supports to size. Drill two angled screw holes in each support, then glue and screw them into place on the stretchers. Use a piece of scrap as a spacer to ensure that all the supports are a consistent ½ in. from the top of the stretchers.

CONNECT FRONT AND BACK. Glue the side stretchers into the back legs, then add the front assembly.

Finish with the Seat

The upholstered seat for this chair begins with a wood foundation. Depending on how firm or soft you want the chair to be, either use a piece of ½-in. plywood or make a hardwood frame with webbing to support the upholstery material. Either way, the base should be the same shape as the perimeter of the top of the seating area.

The seats on most of my chairs have 2 in. of foam wrapped with batting and muslin, then covered with fabric or leather. Your upholsterer will be able to recommend a cushion construction, too.

FINISH WITH SEAT SUPPORTS. Screw the diagonal supports to the stretchers, then add the padded seat cushion.

CLAMP IT UP. Add clamps as needed. Work on a flat surface and check everything again for square. If the chair seems to wobble, adjust the position of the clamps.

9 CLASSIC ARTS & CRAFTS SIDEBOARD

This piece of furniture was a common feature in Arts & Crafts dining rooms. It has drawers to hold napkins, tablecloths, and silverware, as well as cupboards for trays and serving pieces. The broad top makes an ideal place to arrange a buffet or display the Thanksgiving turkey.

I've scaled this sideboard down slightly from typical Arts & Crafts originals, so it can fit in present-day dining areas. Construction is very simple and straightforward. You'll use the same techniques to laminate the legs and cut the mortise-and-tenon joints as you followed in earlier chapters. You'll simply be working with larger pieces of wood. Earlier chapters have featured numerous photos showing pieces being cut at the tablesaw or worked on with a router, so I won't repeat them here. However, the parts for a large piece like this must go together in a very particular order. That's why you will see numerous photos of both the dry-fit and glue-up.

The plan shows drawers of three different heights. However, you can make them identical in height, which will save some time when cutting the dovetail joints for the drawers. Although

(Continued on p. 120)

SIDEBOARD

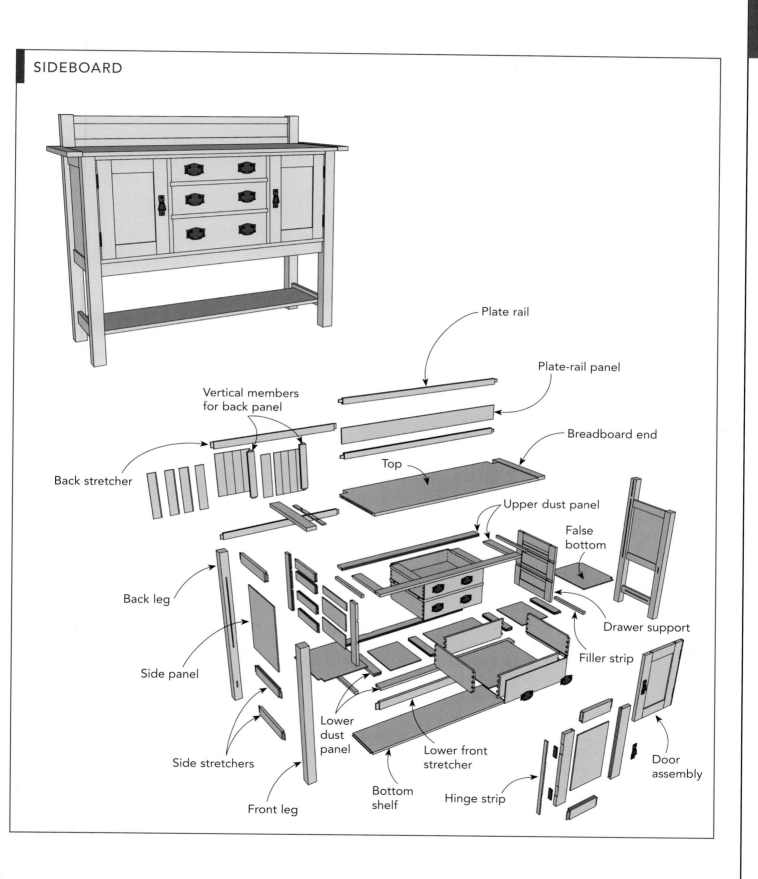

Plate rail

Plate-rail panel

Vertical members
for back panel

Breadboard end

Back stretcher

Top

Upper dust panel

False
bottom

Back leg

Drawer support

Side panel

Filler strip

Side stretchers

Lower
dust
panel

Lower front
stretcher

Door
assembly

Front leg

Bottom
shelf

Hinge strip

QUANTITY	PART	THICKNESS*	WIDTH*	LENGTH*	MATERIAL
2	Front legs	2¼	2¼	39	Quartersawn white oak
2	Back legs	2¼	2¼	46	Quartersawn white oak
6	Side stretchers	¾	2½	15	Quartersawn white oak
2	Side panels	¼	13½	17½	Quartersawn white oak
2	Plate rails	¾	1½	48	Quartersawn white oak
1	Plate rail panel	¼	4	47	Quartersawn white oak
3	Front/back stretchers	¾	2½	48	Quartersawn white oak
2	Vertical member for back panels	¾	2½	18	Quartersawn white oak
4	Shiplap panels	¼	4	18	Quartersawn white oak
8	Shiplap panels	¼	3⅝	18	Quartersawn white oak
1	Bottom shelf	¾	11	49½	Quartersawn white oak
1	Lower dust panel front member	¾	2½	46	Quartersawn white oak
1	Lower dust panel back member	¾	2½	46	Secondary wood
2	Lower dust panel center members	¾	2½	12⅛	Secondary wood
2	Lower dust panel end members	¾	2½	12⅛	Secondary wood
2	Lower dust panel end fillers	¼	10¼	12⅛	Secondary wood
1	Lower dust panel center filler	¼	12⅛	18½	Secondary wood
2	Lower dust panel filler strips	¾	1½	13	Secondary wood
1	Upper dust panel back member	¾	2½	46	Secondary wood
1	Upper dust panel front member	¾	2½	46	Quartersawn white oak
4	Upper dust panel short members	¾	2½	11⅞	Secondary wood
2	Upper dust panel filler strip	¾	1¼	13	Secondary wood
2	Drawer support front stiles	¾	2½	18	Quartersawn white oak

* Measurements are in inches.

QUANTITY	PART	THICKNESS*	WIDTH*	LENGTH*	MATERIAL
2	Drawer support back stiles	¾	2½	18	Secondary wood
6	Drawer support rails	¾	2½	12⅛	Secondary wood
2	Drawer support top panels	¼	2⅛	12⅛	Secondary wood
2	Drawer support center panels	¼	4¾	12⅛	Secondary wood
2	Drawer support bottom panels	¼	4⅛	12⅛	Secondary wood
2	Drawer divider front members	¾	2¼	19¾	Quartersawn white oak
2	Drawer divider back members	¾	2¼	19¾	Secondary wood
4	Drawer divider side members	¾	2¼	12⅛	Secondary wood
2	Drawer divider panels	¼	12⅛	16¼	Secondary wood
1	Top drawer back	½	3¾	19¼	Secondary wood
1	Top drawer false front	¼	4½	19¼	Quartersawn white oak
1	Top drawer front	½	4½	19¼	Quartersawn white oak
2	Top drawer sides	½	4½	15⅝	Secondary wood
1	Center drawer back	½	4⅝	19¼	Secondary wood
1	Center drawer false front	¼	5½	19¼	Quartersawn white oak
1	Center drawer front	½	5½	19¼	Quartersawn white oak
2	Center drawer sides	½	5½	15⅝	Secondary wood
1	Bottom drawer back	½	5⅝	19¼	Secondary wood
1	Bottom drawer false front	¼	6½	19¼	Quartersawn white oak
1	Bottom drawer front	½	6½	19¼	Quartersawn white oak
2	Bottom drawer sides	½	6½	15⅝	Secondary wood
3	Drawer bottoms	¼	15⅜	18¾	Secondary wood
4	Door stiles	¾	2½	18	Quartersawn white oak
2	Door panels	¼	8⅜	14	Quartersawn white oak

* Measurements are in inches.

QUANTITY	PART	THICKNESS*	WIDTH*	LENGTH*	MATERIAL
4	Door rails	3/4	2½	8⅜	Quartersawn white oak
2	Hinge strips	¼	3/4	18	Quartersawn white oak
2	Cupboard false bottoms	¼	15⅜	13⅝	Quartersawn white oak
1	Top	3/4	18½	50½	Quartersawn white oak
8	Splines	¼	1	3	Secondary wood
2	Breadboard ends	3/4	2½	18⅝	Quartersawn white oak

Total board feet: 39

* Measurements are in inches.

HARDWARE

2	Door pulls	6	Drawer pulls
2	Bullet catches	4	Hinges

you can make the sideboard from cherry or mahogany, I think it looks best when made from quartersawn white oak.

Build the Legs First

Mill a dozen pieces of oak to ¾-in. thickness and 2-in. width. Cut them to a rough length (greater than 46 in. for the back legs; greater than 39 in. for the front) and glue them together in four groups of three, just as you did to make the leg laminations for the bed in chapter 5.

If you don't have lots of clamps to use for the leg laminations, you can make a curved caul to get the most from the clamps you do own. Take a 4-ft. length of 2x4 construction lumber and run each end over the jointer two or three times. The clamps will draw the ends of the caul against the workpiece and help spread the pressure.

While you wait for the glue to cure, resaw thin pieces of oak veneer to cover the glue joints. (See chapter 6 for details on resawing.) Make them a bit more than ⅛ in. thick. Scrape off any squeeze-out from the initial glue-up, then glue on the veneers.

Bring the legs to their final size at the planer. Begin by planing the faces without veneer to a hair thicker than 2¼ in. Then flip the legs 90 degrees and bring the veneered faces to their final 2¼-in. thickness. Flip the legs over after each pass to be sure you remove equal amounts from opposite faces. Finally, flip the legs 90 degrees again and take one last pass, making the legs square. At the tablesaw, cut the legs to their final lengths. Use a stop block to ensure that each pair of legs is identical.

Following the plan on the facing page, use a router with an edge guide and a spiral upcut bit to cut all the mortises in the legs. Reset the depth of cut—but don't change the edge-guide setting—to cut shallow grooves between some of the mortises for the ¼-in.-thick side panels.

LEG AND SIDE-PANEL ASSEMBLIES

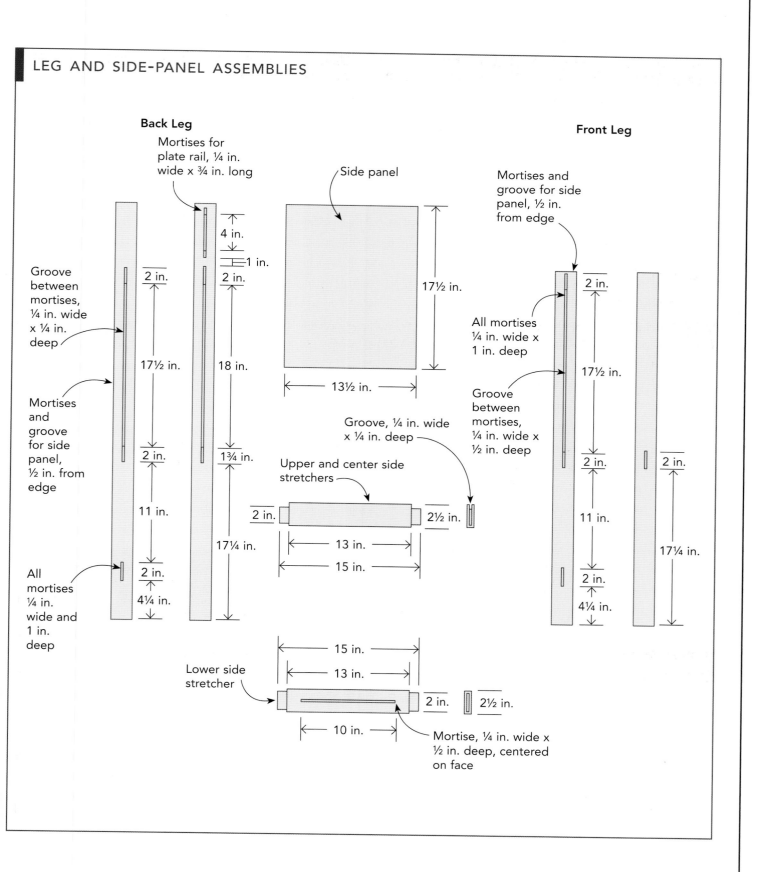

Back Leg

Mortises for plate rail, ¼ in. wide x ¾ in. long

Side panel

Front Leg

Mortises and groove for side panel, ½ in. from edge

4 in.

1 in.

2 in.

2 in.

17½ in.

2 in.

Groove between mortises, ¼ in. wide x ¼ in. deep

17½ in.

18 in.

All mortises ¼ in. wide x 1 in. deep

Mortises and groove for side panel, ½ in. from edge

13½ in.

17½ in.

Groove between mortises, ¼ in. wide x ½ in. deep

2 in.

1¾ in.

2 in.

2 in.

Groove, ¼ in. wide x ¼ in. deep

11 in.

11 in.

Upper and center side stretchers

2 in.

2½ in.

13 in.

15 in.

17¼ in.

2 in.

4¼ in.

All mortises ¼ in. wide and 1 in. deep

2 in.

4¼ in.

17¼ in.

15 in.

13 in.

Lower side stretcher

2 in.

2½ in.

10 in.

Mortise, ¼ in. wide x ½ in. deep, centered on face

ROUTER WORK. Use a router with an edge guide to cut all the mortises in the legs. Then, without changing the edge-guide setting, cut the grooves between mortises to house the side panels.

Mill the Parts for the Carcase

As the plan and cutlist show, you need six short side stretchers and five long front and back stretchers. (Two of those long stretchers are narrower than the others and form the plate rail.) You also need two vertical members that fit between the wider back stretchers, plus the panel for the plate rail and the wide bottom shelf.

When you have all those parts milled to their final dimensions, cut the tenons on the ends, using a dado set in the tablesaw. (As the plans show, the vertical members for the back panel have ½-in.-long tenons; the other tenons are 1 in. long.) Use a rasp to round over the ends of the long tenons so they fit the mortises in the legs.

Four of the side stretchers and the two wider back stretchers have a groove on one edge to house thin panels. Cut those grooves with a router or a dado set in the tablesaw.

To make the side panels, resaw pieces of white oak, bookmatch the pieces, and glue them together (see chapter 6). For the back panels, take thin, narrow pieces of oak and cut rabbets

SHAPING TENONS. Install a dado set in the tablesaw to cut the tenons on the long and short stretchers. Use a stop block to ensure that all the tenons are a uniform length.

STRETCHER DETAILS

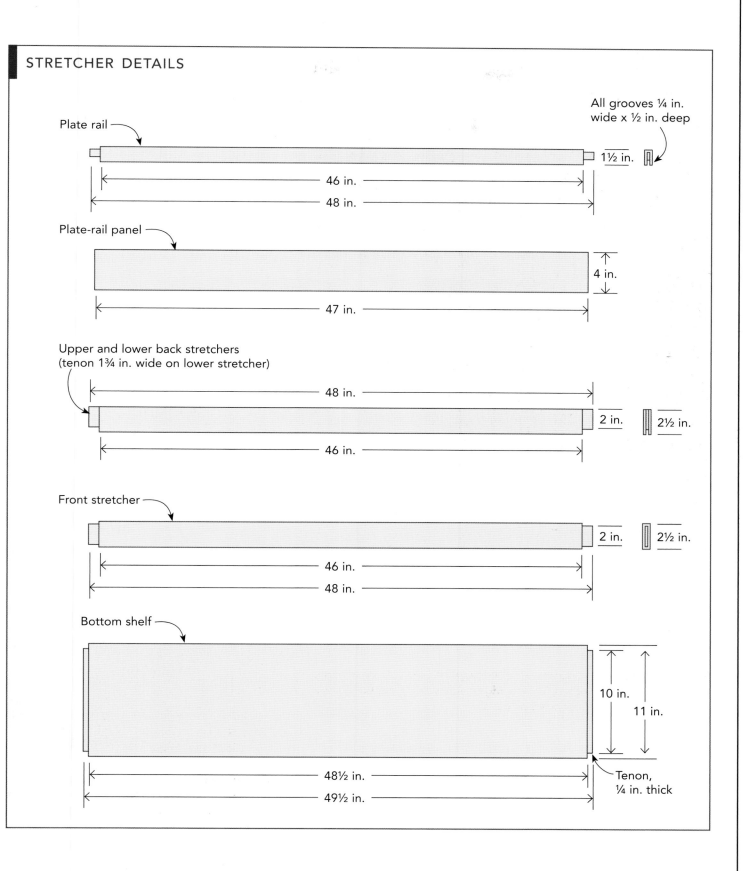

Plate rail

All grooves ¼ in. wide x ½ in. deep

1½ in.

46 in.

48 in.

Plate-rail panel

4 in.

47 in.

Upper and lower back stretchers
(tenon 1¾ in. wide on lower stretcher)

48 in.

2 in.

2½ in.

46 in.

Front stretcher

2 in.

2½ in.

46 in.

48 in.

Bottom shelf

10 in.

11 in.

Tenon,
¼ in. thick

48½ in.

49½ in.

CUT AND FLIP. Once you have cut one face of a tenon, flip the board over to cut the second face. You can also cut the grooves for the panels at the tablesaw.

on opposite faces to shiplap the pieces (see chapter 4). The plan on the facing page shows fixed sizes for the shiplap. However, you can just as easily use boards of random widths; it all depends on what you have in the shop. Because a sideboard is usually against a wall, the shiplap will seldom be seen.

Assemble the back panel, applying glue only to the mortises and tenons on the frame members; don't get glue on the shiplap panels, so they can expand and contract with seasonal changes in humidity.

ROUNDING OVER. Use a rasp to round over the tenons to fit the router-cut mortises. That's faster and easier than squaring the ends of each mortise with a chisel.

SLIP IN SHIPLAP. Slide the thin shiplap panels into the grooves in the back stretchers.

GLUE UP. To complete the back panel, glue and clamp the vertical members that fit into the back stretchers, but don't get glue on the shiplap panels.

BACK-PANEL ASSEMBLY

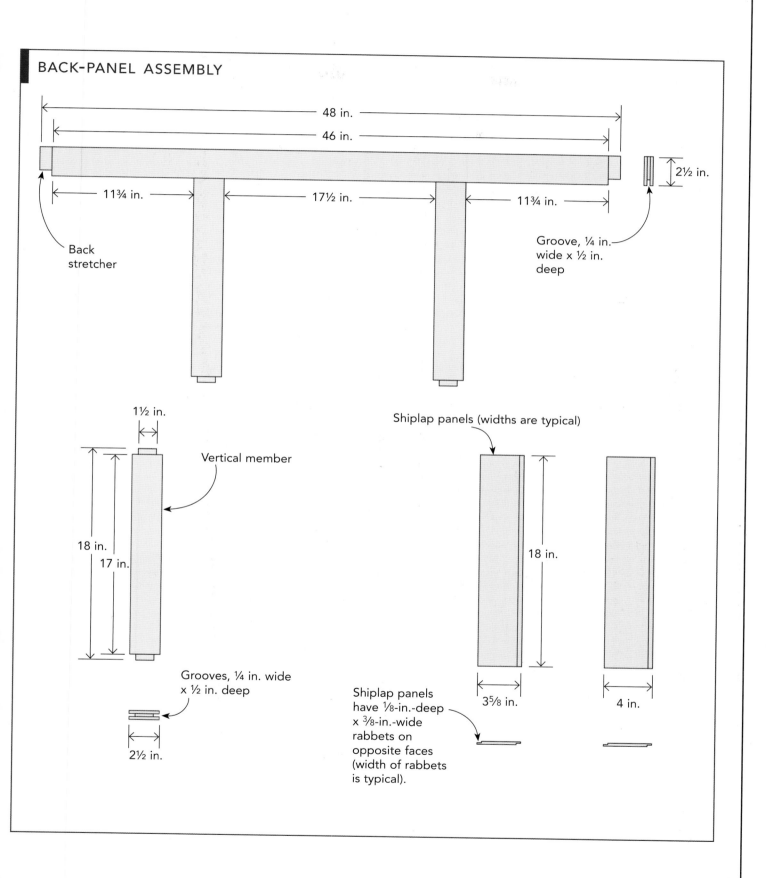

48 in.

46 in.

2½ in.

11¾ in.

17½ in.

11¾ in.

Back stretcher

Groove, ¼ in. wide x ½ in. deep

1½ in.

Vertical member

Shiplap panels (widths are typical)

18 in.

17 in.

18 in.

Grooves, ¼ in. wide x ½ in. deep

2½ in.

Shiplap panels have ⅛-in.-deep x ⅜-in.-wide rabbets on opposite faces (width of rabbets is typical).

3⅝ in.

4 in.

Test the Fit

Do a dry fit of the sideboard now, which will help you rehearse the actual glue-up and make it easier to finish the remaining assemblies.

This is the dry-fit sequence to follow: Fit the side stretchers into one of the back legs. Slide in a side panel, then attach the front leg. Put the lower back stretcher in place and slide in the back panel. Add the stretchers and panel for the plate rail. Assemble the second side and slide it in place. Put the wide bottom shelf in last. Lightly clamp the carcase together and check everything for square. Once you've made sure everything is right, give yourself a pat on the back. You've finished the hard part of this project.

DRY FIT. Clamp the main carcase pieces together to check for fit and square. This dry fit will also make it easier to construct the dust panels and drawer supports.

Make More Panels

Two nearly identical dust panels form the top and bottom of the area for the drawers and cupboards. Because most of these assemblies will never show, they are made from a combination of oak and a secondary wood like poplar. (The front frame members do show and so are made from oak.) As you can see from the plan on the facing page, each frame member for the lower dust panel has a groove that's ½ in. deep and ¼ in. wide to house thin pieces of plywood. The shorter members have stub tenons that fit into the grooves. It's the same type of construction used for the nightstand door (see chapter 6). The upper panel is just the frame, with no plywood in between.

There are more panel assemblies for the drawer dividers and supports. The dimensions of the frame members and panels are different; otherwise, they're made the same way as the larger dust panels.

Begin the panel assemblies by milling batches of boards. The frame members for all the panels are ¾ in. thick, so plane all the pieces to thickness at the same time. Then rip all the frame members of a given width at the same time. Wait to cut pieces to their final length, however.

DUST PANEL GROOVES. Use the tablesaw to make the grooves in the dust-panel frame members. Make the first cut, flip the board around, and make the second cut. This ensures that the groove is centered on the edge of the board.

DUST-PANEL ASSEMBLIES

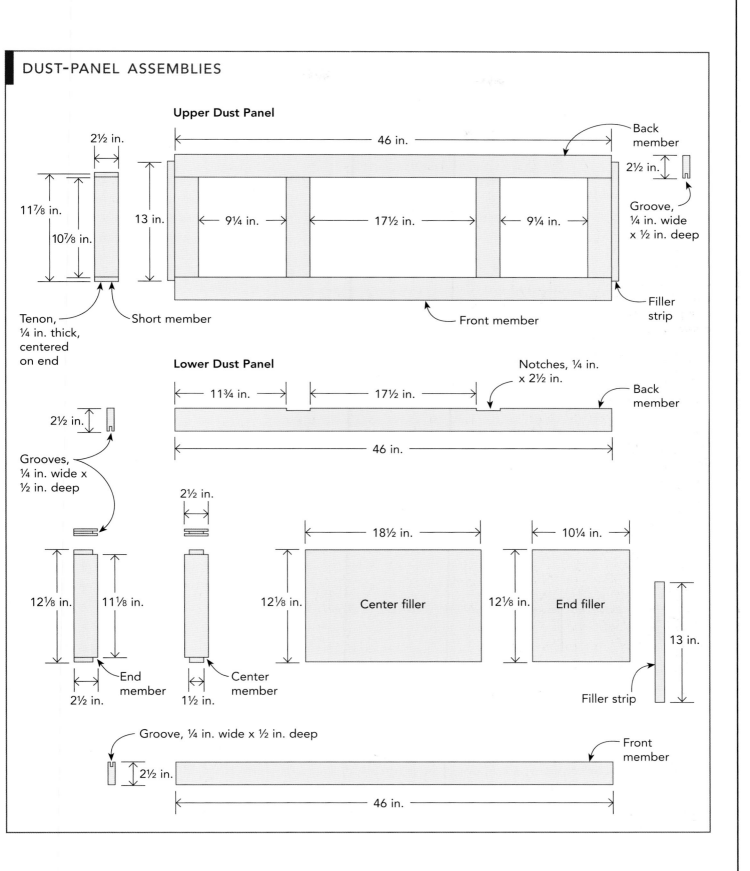

Upper Dust Panel

46 in.

Back member

2½ in.

Groove, ¼ in. wide x ½ in. deep

2½ in.

11⅞ in.

10⅞ in.

13 in.

9¼ in.

17½ in.

9¼ in.

Filler strip

Tenon, ¼ in. thick, centered on end

Short member

Front member

Lower Dust Panel

11¾ in.

17½ in.

Notches, ¼ in. x 2½ in.

Back member

2½ in.

46 in.

Grooves, ¼ in. wide x ½ in. deep

2½ in.

18½ in.

10¼ in.

12⅛ in.

11⅛ in.

12⅛ in.

Center filler

12⅛ in.

End filler

13 in.

2½ in.

End member

Center member

Filler strip

1½ in.

Groove, ¼ in. wide x ½ in. deep

2½ in.

46 in.

Front member

NIBBLE NOTCHES.
One long member for the lower dust panel has to be notched to fit against the back panel. Use the tablesaw to cut the notches, making repeated passes to nibble away the waste.

At the tablesaw, cut the grooves on the edges of the panel members. The outside members have a groove on one edge; center members, a groove on each edge. After you make one cut, flip the board around and make a second cut; this ensures that the groove is centered on the edge.

FINISH THE LARGE DUST PANELS

Cut the short frame members to their final length, following the dimensions on the plan. Use a stop block on the tablesaw. For the long members, use the dry-fit carcase to get the exact measurement. Cut one end square. Hold that end against the inside edge of a leg and use a marking knife to score the wood exactly where it meets the inside edge of the opposite leg. Once you have the length, set up a stop block to make all the long members uniform. Next, cut the stub tenons on all the short frame members. Do this at the tablesaw.

Dry-fit the lower dust panel and take the measurements for the thin panels directly from the frame. Cut and fit the panels; here, it's all right to use 1/4-in. plywood. The lower dust panel has a pair of notches in the rear, so it can rest on the lower front and rear stretchers and transfer weight and stress to the carcase. Hold the back frame member in place and mark where the vertical members meet it. Then, at the tablesaw, use a ripping blade to cut the notches. The teeth on this sawblade will leave a clean, flat surface.

Glue up the panels, making sure to keep glue away from the thin center panels. Following measurements on the plan, cut filler strips for the ends of the dust panels. Glue them onto the ends of the panels, making sure they are flush with the other frame members.

ADD FILLER STRIPS. Glue filler strips to the ends of the dust panels. When you clamp the strips, be sure they remain in plane with the rest of the dust panel. Clamping pressure can often push pieces out of alignment.

WORK SMART

While a pencil works just fine for marking cutlines and some layout lines, it isn't perfect. Sometimes, you need a thinner line than even the sharpest pencil can deliver. That's when to use a marking knife. It doesn't have to be fancy—a utility knife from the hardware store or an X-ACTO knife from a craft store will do the job.

MAKE THE DRAWER SUPPORTS AND DIVIDERS

Cut the components for the vertical drawer supports to length and add a groove for the thin panels. In the same way, cut the horizontal

DRAWER SUPPORT ASSEMBLIES

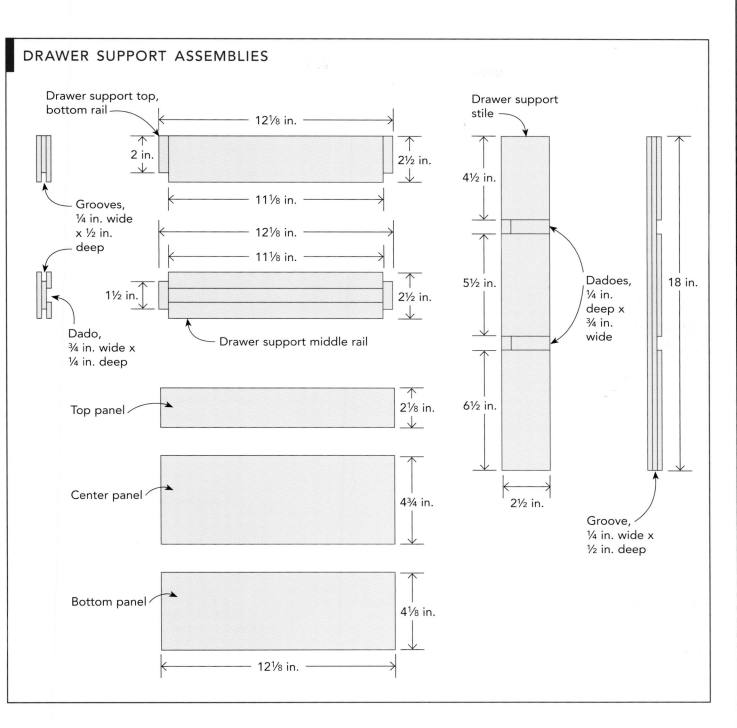

Drawer support top, bottom rail

12⅛ in.

2 in.

2½ in.

11⅛ in.

Grooves, ¼ in. wide x ½ in. deep

12⅛ in.

11⅛ in.

1½ in.

2½ in.

Dado, ¾ in. wide x ¼ in. deep

Drawer support middle rail

Top panel

2⅛ in.

Center panel

4¾ in.

Bottom panel

4⅛ in.

12⅛ in.

Drawer support stile

4½ in.

5½ in.

Dadoes, ¼ in. deep x ¾ in. wide

18 in.

6½ in.

2½ in.

Groove, ¼ in. wide x ½ in. deep

frame members for the drawer dividers, add a groove to each one, and cut their thin panels to size.

Make the two drawer-support assemblies. Glue the horizontal members into one vertical member. When the glue has dried, dry-fit the second vertical member in place and plow a pair of shallow dadoes to house the drawer dividers. Then finish assembling the vertical supports.

ASSEMBLE DRAWER SUPPORTS. The vertical supports use frame-and-panel construction. Before final glue-up, cut the dadoes that house the dividers.

ASSEMBLE DRAWER DIVIDERS. The horizontal drawer dividers go together the same way the dust panels do. The front piece for the divider is made of quartersawn oak; the others, from a secondary wood.

ASSEMBLE THE DRAWER DIVIDERS

Cut the front and back frame members for the drawer dividers, following the measurements on the cutlist (and the plan on p. 129). Cut the remaining frame members and the thin center panels. Assemble the dividers as you have all the others. Then glue them into the dadoes in the vertical supports. Be sure to check this assembly for square very carefully; otherwise, the drawers will not fit neatly.

SLIP IN A PANEL. Once you have glued up three frame members, slide a thin piece of plywood into the grooves.

SUBASSEMBLY GLUE-UP. Fit the horizontal drawer dividers into the dadoes in the vertical supports. It may seem obvious, but be sure the oak pieces line up.

TAP IN PLACE. Give the assembly a few blows with a deadblow mallet to be sure the dividers are well seated in their dadoes.

CLAMP AND CHECK. Clamp the drawer subassembly and carefully check that everything is square. If pieces are off even a little, the drawers may not fit properly.

Make the Doors

Choose the wood for the door frames carefully, looking for pieces with beautiful straight grain and figure. Arrange the pieces carefully, too, to get the grain orientation just right.

Take the measurements for the frame pieces directly from the dry-fit case; the measurements on the plan and cutlist are probably close, but it's safer to work directly from the sideboard you're building. Be sure to add 1 in. to the length of the rails (the horizontal pieces) to allow for the tenons.

Mill all the parts at once, jointing and planing them to their ¾-in. thickness. Rip the pieces to width and cut them to length. Cut a ¼-in.-wide groove ½ in. deep in all the frame pieces. Then cut the tenons in the rails.

Resaw and bookmatch thin pieces for the door panels, and glue them up. Once the glue dries, rip and crosscut the panels to their final size. When ripping to width, be sure to keep the glue line centered (see pp. 68–69).

Glue-up for the doors is exactly the same as it was for the dust panels. Here, too, be sure to keep glue away from the center panels.

DOOR ASSEMBLIES

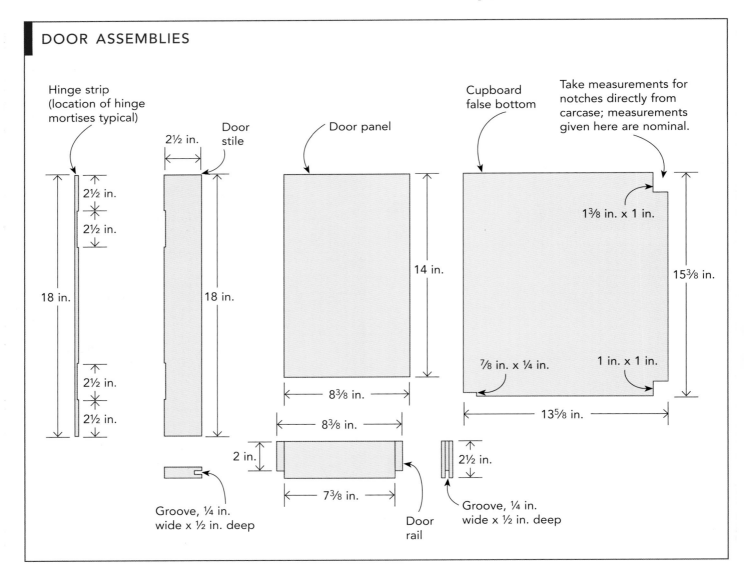

DRAWER COMPONENTS

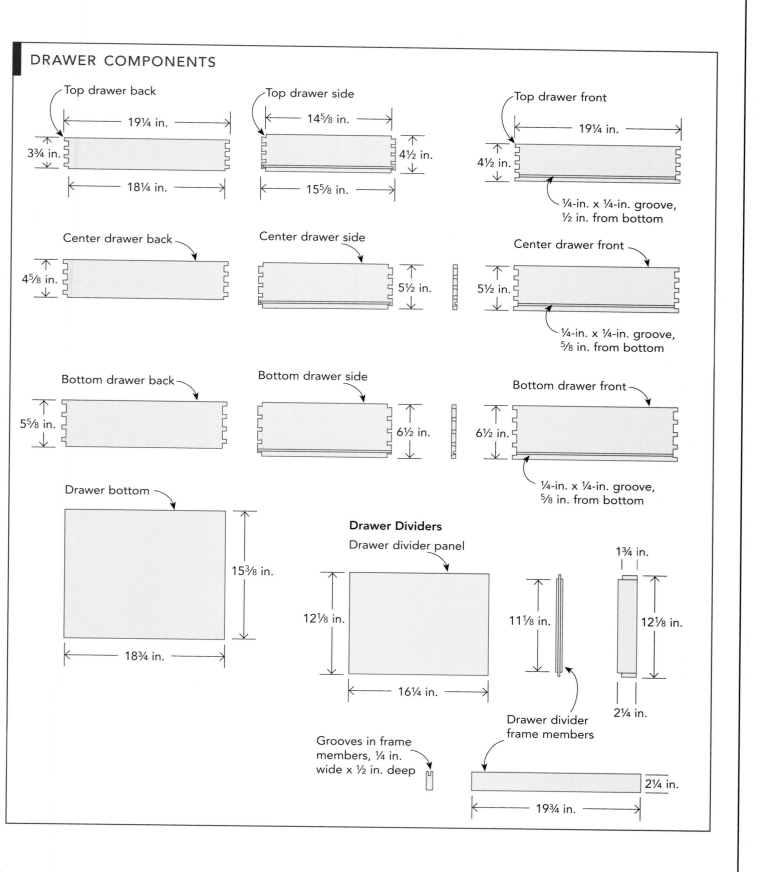

Top drawer back

19¼ in.

3¾ in.

18¼ in.

Top drawer side

14⅝ in.

4½ in.

15⅝ in.

Top drawer front

19¼ in.

4½ in.

¼-in. x ¼-in. groove,
½ in. from bottom

Center drawer back

4⅝ in.

Center drawer side

5½ in.

Center drawer front

5½ in.

¼-in. x ¼-in. groove,
⅝ in. from bottom

Bottom drawer back

5⅝ in.

Bottom drawer side

6½ in.

Bottom drawer front

6½ in.

¼-in. x ¼-in. groove,
⅝ in. from bottom

Drawer bottom

15⅜ in.

18¾ in.

Drawer Dividers

Drawer divider panel

12⅛ in.

16¼ in.

11⅛ in.

1¾ in.

12⅛ in.

2¼ in.

Drawer divider
frame members

Grooves in frame
members, ¼ in.
wide x ½ in. deep

2¼ in.

19¾ in.

Dovetail the Drawers

At first glance, the three drawers in the sideboard seem to have half-blind dovetail joints at the front. They are actually through dovetails—a simpler joint to make—camouflaged to look like half-blinds. As a result, you can do all the joinery for the drawers at the tablesaw. (The drawer back is joined to the sides with through dovetails that are identical to those for the front.)

Mill the stock for the drawer sides, backs, and fronts in batches, following the measurements on the cutlist (and the plan on p. 133). Make the fronts from oak; the other parts can be a secondary wood. Also resaw pieces of nicely figured straight-grain oak to use as a false front; see the cutlist for dimensions. You can use plywood for the drawer bottoms.

LAY OUT THE TAILS

Scribe the baseline of the tails on both ends of the drawer sides. Set a bevel gauge for a 10-degree angle and use it to lay out the tails, spacing them however you like. (The plan below shows just one arrangement.) Whatever the spacing, the layout should be symmetrical and centered on the drawer side. Be sure to make an X in the waste areas so you don't cut the wrong part of the board. Don't change the setting on the bevel gauge.

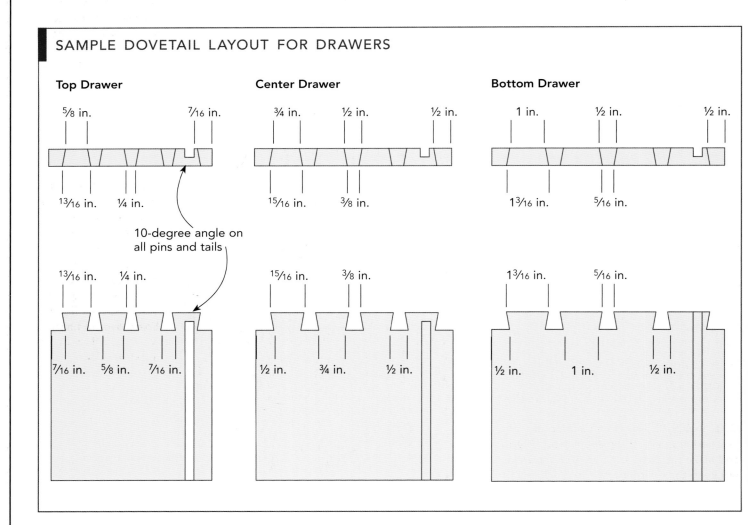

SAMPLE DOVETAIL LAYOUT FOR DRAWERS

Top Drawer

5/8 in.   7/16 in.

13/16 in.   1/4 in.

10-degree angle on all pins and tails

13/16 in.   1/4 in.

7/16 in.   5/8 in.   7/16 in.

Center Drawer

3/4 in.   1/2 in.   1/2 in.

15/16 in.   3/8 in.

15/16 in.   3/8 in.

1/2 in.   3/4 in.   1/2 in.

Bottom Drawer

1 in.   1/2 in.   1/2 in.

13/16 in.   5/16 in.

13/16 in.   5/16 in.

1/2 in.   1 in.   1/2 in.

CUT THE TAILS

Use a rip blade for the dovetail cuts. Make the tails first. Use the bevel gauge to set the blade angle at 10 degrees. Set the blade height just a hair below the baseline for the tails (use a piece of scrap to check this). Then make a cut through the jig; you'll use this to align the drawer side for successive cuts.

Align the outermost layout line with the kerf in the jig. Clamp a stop block against the opposite side of the workpiece. Make a cut through the drawer side, then flip the board around and make another cut. Repeat for the second drawer side. Flip the board around again and align the next layout line with the kerf in the jig. Move the stop block. Make two more cuts. Repeat the process until you've cut all the tails on both drawer sides.

Clamp a drawer side to the bench and carefully chisel away the waste. Hold the chisel slightly away from the line marking the base of the tails. Chop about half-way through the board, then flip it over and finish chopping from the other side.

Dovetail Jig

Make a tablesaw jig for dovetailing. Glue and screw a piece of ¼-in. plywood to a piece of ¾-in. plywood; see the photo at bottom left. The actual size of the pieces isn't important, as long as the jig will support the pieces you have to cut. Screw or clamp the jig to the tablesaw's miter gauge.

ALL-PURPOSE ANGLE. Set a bevel gauge for 10 degrees. Use it to lay out the dovetail tails and to set the angle of the tablesaw blade to begin cutting the tails.

CUT AND FLIP. Align one mark on the drawer side with the saw kerf in the jig and make the cut. Flip the board around and make the same cut from the opposite face. A stop block will keep the board aligned for each pair of cuts.

CHISEL AWAY THE WASTE. Once you've made all the cuts at the tablesaw, use a chisel to pare away the waste at the top of the cuts. Chisel part-way through on one side, then flip the board over to finish the cuts. This helps to avoid tearout.

ANGLE THE JIG TO CUT THE PINS. Angle the miter fence and jig 10 degrees to cut the pins. Don't change the height of the sawblade.

CUT AND NIBBLE. Make a series of cuts to nibble away the waste between pins. You may need to use a chisel to clear away all the waste.

A FINE FIT. Cutting dovetails on the tablesaw goes quickly. And if everything works right, you shouldn't have to do much fine-tuning with a chisel to get a nice, tight-fitting joint.

FAKING A JOINT. Glue a thin piece of oak over the drawer front to create the illusion of a half-blind dovetail joint. A caul (a piece of melamine-faced plywood) spreads the clamping pressure evenly.

USE THE TAILS TO LAY OUT THE PINS

Clamp a drawer front in the bench vise and rest a drawer side on top of it. Use a marking knife or a mechanical pencil with a very fine line to mark the location of the pins. Then use a square to transfer the lines to the faces of the board.

Set the sawblade angle to 90 degrees. Use the bevel gauge to angle the miter gauge 10 degrees. Align the workpiece with the kerf in the jig, clamp the stop block in place, and make your first cut. Move the workpiece to the next layout line, set the stop block, and make the second cut.

When you've made all the cuts you can at that angle, reset the miter gauge so it's angled 10 degrees in the opposite direction. Make the remaining cuts to establish the edges of the pins. You can make a series of cuts to nibble away most of the waste. However, you'll either have to reset the miter gauge or use a chisel to pare away all the waste. Repeat until you've cut all the pins in the drawer front and back.

TEST THE FIT

See how well the drawer fronts and sides fit together. Use a chisel to remove very thin slivers from either the pins or tails until the pieces fit together snugly, without needing too much pressure (much less a whack from a mallet).

Cut a 1/4-in. dado in all the pieces to house the drawer bottom. Slide the bottom into its groove and glue up the drawer box. As always, make sure it's square and sits flat.

ADD THE FALSE FRONT

Tap a couple of brads into the drawer front and cut them off nearly flush with the wood. Apply glue to the thick veneer you resawed earlier and press the veneer onto the drawer. Clamp it in place. The brads prevent the veneer from shifting out of position when you tighten the clamps.

SIDES FIRST. Begin assembling the sideboard by gluing up the two side assemblies.

POSITION THE CLAMPS. Center the clamps over the stretchers. Be sure to check everything for square.

Add the Top

Following the measurements on the cutlist, mill and glue up pieces for the top. Once the glue has cured and you've removed any squeeze-out, cut the top to its final width and length.

Use a router to cut a groove that's ¼ in. wide and ½ in. deep in the ends of the top and on one edge of each breadboard end. Stop the grooves about 1 in. from each end; don't cut the grooves the full length of these boards. This technique is also used on the Greene & Greene writing desk in chapter 7.

Mill a piece of secondary wood to be ¼ in. thick and 1 in. wide, and cut it into short lengths; these will be used as splines to join the breadboard ends to the top. Fit them into the grooves in the top, but glue only the center spline. Then glue the breadboard end in place.

Glue up in Stages

Gluing up and assembling the sideboard is a process that extends over three days. Follow the sequence here.

Begin with the side assemblies. Let the glue cure overnight.

For the next stage of glue-up, use an adhesive with an extended open time, such as Titebond® III. Put some scrap 4x4s on the floor and rest one of the side assemblies on them. It will be easier to work this way instead of on a bench. Fit the rear panel into its mortises. Next, fit the wide bottom shelf into its mortise. Fit the stretchers and panel for the plate rail into place. Attach the long front stretcher. Once all the rails and panels are in place, fit the second side assembly in place over the mortises on the rails.

Pivot the entire carcase right-side up. Apply all the clamps you need, but don't tighten them fully yet. Check the case for square, then tighten the clamps. Again, let the glue cure overnight.

WORK ON THE FLOOR. Rest one side assembly on scrap blocks on the floor, then fit the back panel into its mortises.

ADD A STRETCHER. With the back panel in place, glue in the wide bottom stretcher.

NEXT, THE PLATE RAIL. Fit the two plate-rail stretchers in their mortises, then slide in the panel that fits between them.

TAP IN THE LOWER FRONT RAIL. Install this rail next. You may need to tap it with a deadblow mallet to seat it firmly.

ADD THE SECOND SIDE. Fit the second side assembly in place over the long stretchers. Then clamp up the sideboard and make sure everything remains square.

Next day, slide the lower dust panel into position. Secure it with screws driven from the bottom of the front stretcher. Next, attach the drawer-support assembly in place. Take care to get it into exactly the right position. Screw through the lower dust panel into the vertical supports.

Attach the upper dust panel, using glue on the ends of the filler strips and screws driven through the short frame members and into the drawer-support assembly. Clamp the upper panel to the side assemblies. Before you tighten the clamps, be sure the dust panel aligns with the top of the front legs and the upper side rails.

Slide the top into position and hold it in place with screws driven up through the upper dust panel.

PLACE THE LOWER DUST PANEL. This panel rests on the lower front and rear stretchers as well as the two lower side stretchers.

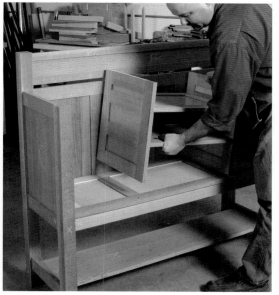

CLAMP AND SCREW. Once you have the drawer support in position, clamp it in place and hold it with screws driven through the lower dust panel.

SCREW IT DOWN. Drive two screws into the lower front stretcher to hold the dust panel in place. The drawer supports will hide the screws.

NOW FOR THE DRAWER SUPPORT. Position the drawer-support assembly. Be sure it's centered left to right.

PLACE THE UPPER DUST PANEL. This part of the sideboard rests atop the drawer support and aligns with the top of the front legs and side assemblies.

Resaw and bookmatch pieces for the thin false bottoms in the cupboards. Cut them to size. The cutlist and the plan on p. 132 give nominal dimensions, but it's best to take measurements directly from the carcase. Notch the panels to fit around the legs. Slide them into place in the cupboard openings.

Attach the thin filler strips to the front legs, on the outer edges of the cupboard spaces. These fillers provide clearance for the hinges and keep the doors from binding.

Fit the drawers into their openings. Plane the top and sides as needed so the drawers slide smoothly.

GLUE THE ENDS. Glue and clamp the filler strips on the upper dust panel to the top side stretcher.

ADD SOME SCREWS. Drive screws through the upper dust panel into the vertical drawer supports to help hold everything together.

POSITION THE TOP. The top, with its breadboard ends, is the last part of the carcase to go in place.

SIDE ASSEMBLIES

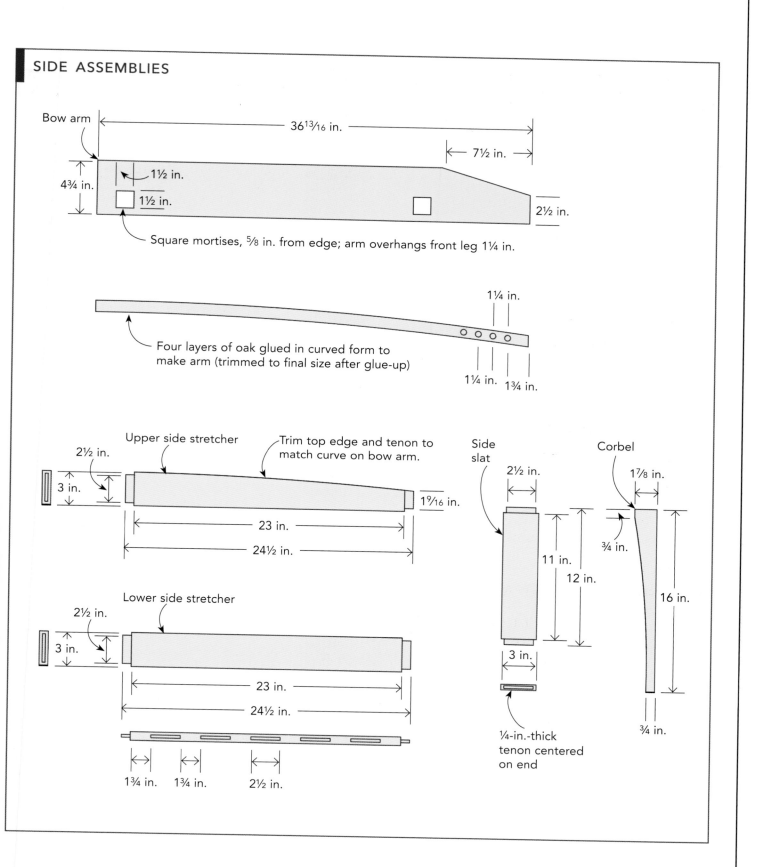

Bow arm

36¹³/₁₆ in.

7½ in.

4¾ in.

1½ in.

1½ in.

2½ in.

Square mortises, ⅝ in. from edge; arm overhangs front leg 1¼ in.

1¼ in.

1¼ in. 1¾ in.

Four layers of oak glued in curved form to make arm (trimmed to final size after glue-up)

Upper side stretcher

Trim top edge and tenon to match curve on bow arm.

2½ in.

3 in.

1⁹/₁₆ in.

23 in.

24½ in.

Side slat

2½ in.

11 in.

12 in.

3 in.

¼-in.-thick tenon centered on end

Corbel

1⅞ in.

¾ in.

16 in.

¾ in.

Lower side stretcher

2½ in.

3 in.

23 in.

24½ in.

1¾ in. 1¾ in. 2½ in.

TRUE THE FORM.
Here, I've attached a second layer of particleboard for the bending form to the first. The bearing on the router bit rides against the curve on the first layer, so the bit cuts the second layer to match it exactly.

LAYER UP. Add additional layers to the form until it's seven layers high. You can screw them together or, as shown here, pin them with a pneumatic nailer.

CUT A SECOND TEMPLATE. Cut a second template for the curve on the arms. You'll use this one to trim the top side stretcher so it fits snugly against the arm.

tom right. Cover the stop, the fence, and the curved edges of the gluing form with packing tape; this will prevent glue from sticking to the form.

ASSEMBLE THE ARMS

Mill four pieces of 4/4 quartersawn oak slightly larger in width and length than the finished arms. Resaw them in half, then plane them to their final ¼-in. thickness. I like to begin the resawing at the tablesaw, running the pieces over the sawblade to make a groove along each long edge. Those grooves help guide the bandsaw blade through the wood.

Choose the pieces with the nicest grain and figure for the top faces of the arms. Use a small paint roller to spread glue evenly on the faces of four boards. Rather than use conventional yellow glue, I prefer urea-formaldehyde adhesive because it allows me more time to assemble the laminations. (It's also a rigid adhesive, which means that the arm won't spring back, or try to straighten out, once it's removed from the form.) Once you've applied the adhesive, stack

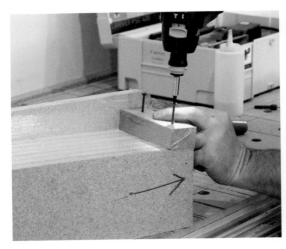

FINISH THE FORM. Screw a fence to one side of the completed bending form and a stop block at one end. Cover the form, the fence, and the stop block with packing tape to prevent the glue from sticking.

BOW-ARM GLUING FORM TEMPLATE

Each square = 1 in.

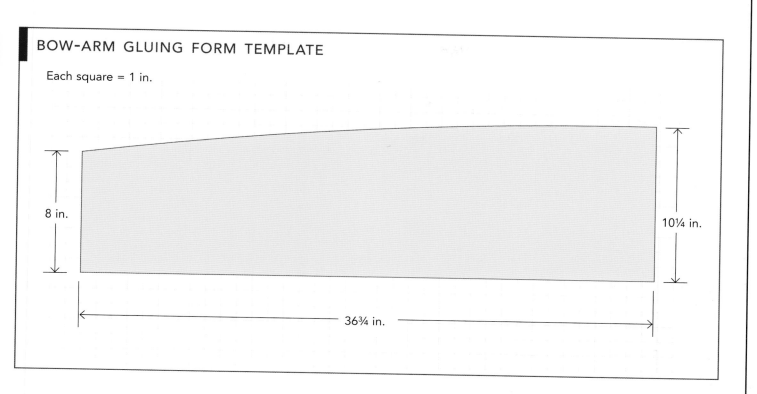

8 in.

10¼ in.

36¾ in.

the pieces and fit them into the gluing form. Be sure one end of each piece fits snug against the stop, and that one edge is snug against the fence.

Finally, put a clamping caul made from three layers of whiteboard on top of the oak, white face down. (Whiteboard, available at most home centers, is ⅛-in. Masonite covered on one side with white glue-resistant thermofoil.) Then begin attaching the clamps. Begin at the stop and work your way backward, with one clamp every 3 in.

CUT THE ARMS TO SIZE

You'll likely have some glue squeeze-out that you will want to remove, but be careful. The dried glue, where it contacted the form, will be razor-sharp. Scrape the glue from one edge of the arm lamination and joint it flat. Then rip the arm to width, running it across the tablesaw blade with the concave side up. To cut the arms to length, use a crosscut sled on the tablesaw.

BEST FACE FORWARD. Examine the boards for the arms carefully. Pick the ones with the best grain and figure for the top. They will go onto the bending form last.

WORK
SAFE

Urea-formaldehyde adhesive is a known carcinogen. When you use it, wear gloves and a respirator, or work in a well-ventilated area.

AN ARMY OF CLAMPS. Stack four pieces for one arm in the bending form, making sure they are snug against the fence and stop. Top with a thin caul to spread clamping pressure, then begin attaching the clamps.

GOBS OF GLUE. I use urea formaldehyde glue for the arm laminations, spreading a uniform layer on each piece with a paint roller.

Shim the leg to get a square cut on the end, and attach a clamp to hold it in place.

Following the measurements on the plan on p. 145, layout out the centerpoints and drill four holes in each arm for the back-adjustment pins. Then, at the bandsaw, cut away the angled portion at the outside rear of each arm.

TRIM THE ARMS. When the glue has dried, joint one side flat. It will register against the tablesaw's rip fence when you trim the arm to its final width.

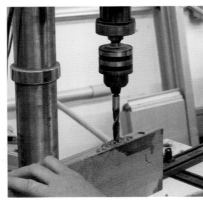

HOLES FOR PINS. Each arm needs four ½-in. holes to house the pins that support the back. Make the holes at the drill press.

FINAL TRIMMING. Go back to the bandsaw to cut away the angled section at the outside rear edge of each arm. For safety, cut with the top of the arm facing up, as shown here.

LEG AND BACK ASSEMBLIES

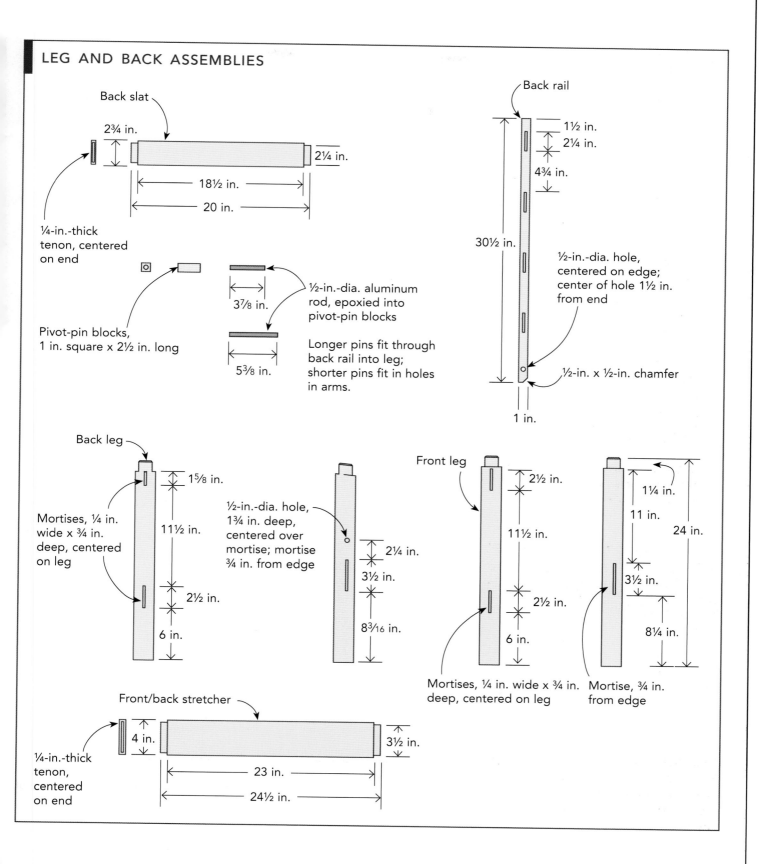

Back slat

2¾ in.

2¼ in.

18½ in.

20 in.

¼-in.-thick tenon, centered on end

Pivot-pin blocks, 1 in. square x 2½ in. long

3⅞ in.

5⅜ in.

½-in.-dia. aluminum rod, epoxied into pivot-pin blocks

Longer pins fit through back rail into leg; shorter pins fit in holes in arms.

Back rail

1½ in.

2¼ in.

4¾ in.

30½ in.

½-in.-dia. hole, centered on edge; center of hole 1½ in. from end

½-in. x ½-in. chamfer

1 in.

Back leg

Mortises, ¼ in. wide x ¾ in. deep, centered on leg

1⅝ in.

11½ in.

2½ in.

6 in.

½-in.-dia. hole, 1¾ in. deep, centered over mortise; mortise ¾ in. from edge

2¼ in.

3½ in.

8³⁄₁₆ in.

Front leg

2½ in.

11½ in.

2½ in.

6 in.

1¼ in.

11 in.

24 in.

3½ in.

8¼ in.

Mortises, ¼ in. wide x ¾ in. deep, centered on leg

Mortise, ¾ in. from edge

Front/back stretcher

4 in.

3½ in.

23 in.

24½ in.

¼-in.-thick tenon, centered on end

Assemble the Sides

Begin by milling the parts for the legs, stretchers, side slats, and decorative corbels. The legs are made by laminating three pieces of ¾-in. stock, then covering the glue joints with a thin veneer. It's the same technique used for the nightstand (p. 61) and the sideboard (p. 116). When you've finished the glue-up, joint and plane the legs to their final thickness, then cut them to length. Wait to cut the square through-tenons on the top end of the legs, however.

I made the chair shown here with loose tenons, but you can of course use conventional mortise-and-tenon joinery instead. If you choose that method, subtract the length of the tenons from the measurements in the cutlist on p. 144.

Follow the measurements on the plan on p. 149 for the position of the mortises. Lay them out on the legs and cut them with a router. (Cut the matching mortises in the stretchers if you're using loose tenons.) Cut five equally spaced mortises, which house the side slats, on one edge of the upper and lower side stretchers. For accuracy, lay out those mortises on all four stretchers at once.

Following the dimensions on the plan on p. 145, cut out the corbels at the bandsaw. Their top ends will need some additional shaping, to fit the curved arm, once you have the sides glued together.

MORE MILLING. Joint and plane the pieces you'll need to make the legs, stretchers, and side slats.

GANG UP THE MORTISES. For accuracy, lay out the location of the mortises in all four legs at once.

CUT THE CORBELS. These elements are partially decorative, partially structural. They do help support the arms. Cut the corbels at the bandsaw.

DRY-FIT AND SHAPE THE STRETCHER

Assemble the sides without glue. Take the template you made earlier from ¼-in. MDF and align its straight edge with the bottom edge of the upper side stretcher. Trace the shape of the curve on the legs. Remove the legs, realign the template with the top stretcher, and trace its curve on the top edge of the stretcher. At the bandsaw, cut the curve on the top side stretchers. Smooth the curves with a block plane or random-orbit sander.

COMPLETE THE LEGS

To shape the square through-tenons on the top of the legs, begin by cutting away most of the waste with a dado set or a tenoning jig on the tablesaw. Cut the front and back shoulders square to the faces. Then use a chisel to chop away the remaining waste, following the curve marked on the side.

Dry-fit the side assemblies again. Following the measurements on the plan on p. 152, mark the 4-degree angle to be cut on the bottom of each leg. (The angle begins at the bottom front corner of the front leg; on the back leg, the angle begins 1½ in. up from the bottom rear corner.) Disassemble the side and remove the legs.

The simplest way to cut the bottom of the legs is with a compound miter saw. Align the sawblade with a mark on a front leg and clamp a stop block to the miter saw's fence. Make the cuts on both front legs. Repeat the process for the back legs.

TIME TO TEST. Dry-fit the side assemblies to check the joinery and ensure that they are square.

MARK THE UPPER STRETCHER. Use the thin curved template to mark the curve on the top side stretcher. Then cut the curve at the bandsaw.

FAIR THE CURVE. Smooth the curved edge of the stretcher with a block plane or sandpaper until the stretcher and arm fit together well.

LAY OUT A SLANT.
Use a long straight-edge to lay out the angled cuts at the bottom of the legs. Take the side assembly apart and cut the legs at a miter saw.

CHOP. Use a compound miter saw to make the angled cuts at the bottom of the legs. Many saws have a laser like the one shown here, which helpfully highlights the cutline.

ANGLE THE LEGS

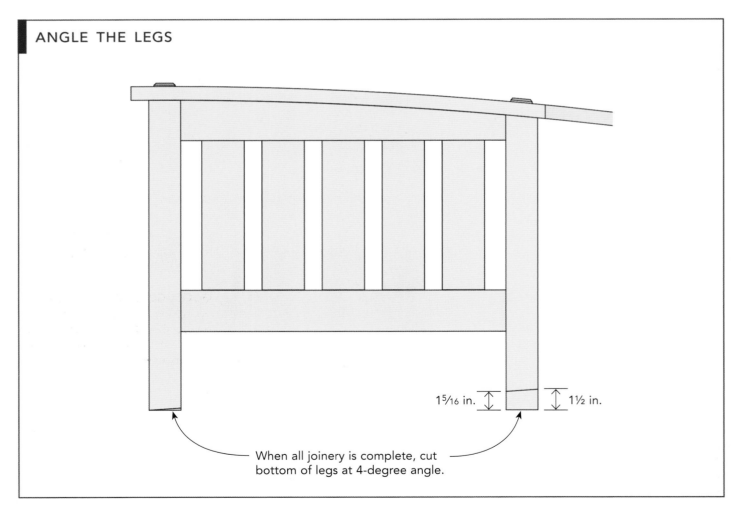

1$\frac{5}{16}$ in.   1½ in.

When all joinery is complete, cut bottom of legs at 4-degree angle.

Mortise the Arms

Put one side assembly back together. Clamp the assembly to the workbench so that the inside of the chair faces the bench and the tenons on the legs overhang the side of the bench. On the underside of each arm, draw a line parallel to the front end and 1¼ in. from that end. This line shows where the arm and front leg meet, and indicates the overhang of the arm.

MARK THE MORTISE LOCATIONS

Take one arm and hold it in place so the 1¼-in. layout line is aligned with the front of the leg and the concave face is tight against the tenons on the legs. From underneath, mark where the front and back faces of the tenons intersect the arm.

Use a combination square and pencil to carry those lines around to the other faces. Then, measuring from the inside edge of the arm, mark the remaining sides of the through mortises. Mark both the top and bottom faces of the arm.

DRILL AND CHISEL

Remove most of the waste in the mortises; drill it out with a Forstner bit or clear it with a router. To avoid tearout, drill or rout about halfway through from one face, then flip the arm over and finish from the opposite face. Clean up the mortises with a chisel. Keep the side walls of the mortises perpendicular to the top and bottom faces of the arm. The front and back mortise walls should be angled to match the angle of the tenons. Test the fit. Aim for the tightest fit on the top face of the arm; the fit on the bottom face can be a little loose.

TRIM AND BEVEL

Trim the tenons so that they are about ¼ in. proud of the top of the arm and parallel to the

MARK THE ARMS. Lay an arm against the legs, with the correct overhang at the front. Trace the position of the legs onto the underside of the arm so you can then lay out the through mortises.

MORE CHOPPING. Drill out most of the waste for the arm mortises, then clean up the holes with a chisel. Aim for the best fit on the top face of the arm.

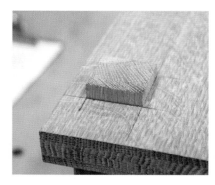

GOOD, CLOSE FIT. If you do everything just right, your through-tenons should look something like this, ready for a small bevel around the top edge.

DOUBLE UP. Keep the two back rails together so you can mark the location of the mortises for the back slats on both rails at once. That helps ensure that the back assembly will go together square.

CLAMP ACROSS THE SLATS. When gluing up the back assembly, center the clamps over the slats, so that clamping pressure pushes squarely against the tenons.

top face of the arm. Use a sharp chisel or block plane to put a shallow bevel on each tenon. Stay above the plane of the arm. Bevels that meet the arm will create a shadow line, which will look like a gap. It's better to let the tenon protrude square for about $1/16$ in., then begin the bevel.

Glue Up the Side Assembly

Slide the side slats into their mortises in the lower side stretcher, then fit the top side stretcher in place. Glue the stretchers into the legs, making sure that the top of the upper stretcher aligns with the tenon shoulders on the legs. Clamp the assembly across the joints for the rails. Run a thin bead of glue over the top of the upper side stretcher and fit the arm over the through-tenons. Clamp the arm with F-style clamps; put the swivel end of the clamp on the arm and the fixed end on the lower side stretcher.

Curve the top edges of the corbels so they conform to the curve of the arms. Use a block plane, a sander, or a chisel for this. When the corbels fit well, glue them in place. With the two sides assembled, glue the front and back stretchers in place. Position the seat cleats $7/8$ in. down from the top of the front and back stretchers, and screw them onto the stretchers.

Make the Back and Pivot Pins

Mill the two back rails to their final size, and cut the mortises in them for the four back slats. Drill the holes for the pivot pins, following the dimensions on the plan on p. 149. Cut a chamfer on the bottom edge of each rail; this prevents the rail from damaging the seat cushion when you tilt the back.

Mill the four slats and cut the tenons on their ends, using a dado set in the tablesaw. Test the fit and plane the tenons as needed. When the slats fit their mortises snugly, glue up the back assembly.

MAKE THE PIVOT PINS

The chair uses two pairs of pins. One pair holds the back in place against the legs and allows the back to swing back and forth. The second pair serves as a stop to hold the back once it has been tilted back. Original Morris chairs typically used turned wood pins. On this version, lengths of aluminum rod take the place of the turnings.

To make the pins, cut four small blocks of oak and drill a ½-in.-dia. hole in each one. Then cut four lengths of ½-in. aluminum rod, following the plan on p. 149. (To hold the aluminum safely, build a jig like the one shown in the sidebar on p. 156. Attach the rods to the blocks of oak with epoxy adhesive.

Slide two pivot pins through the holes at the bottom of the back rails. Then fit the remaining pins into the holes in the arms. That completes the Morris chair construction. All that remains is the creation of the seat frame and cushions.

PIN ASSEMBLY. Hold the aluminum pins in place with epoxy adhesive. Be sure to remove any squeeze-out before the epoxy sets.

FINAL ASSEMBLY. Use the aluminum pivot pins to hold the back in place.

V-Block Jig

You can cut aluminum with regular woodworking blades, but you need to hold the metal securely. Make a jig like the one shown here. I used a V-groove router bit to cut the pieces that clamp over the aluminum. Screw one grooved piece to a base. Hold the other one in place with a toggle clamp.

BAR STOCK HOLDER. Make a jig like this to secure the aluminum rod so that the force of the sawblade doesn't pick up and throw the metal.

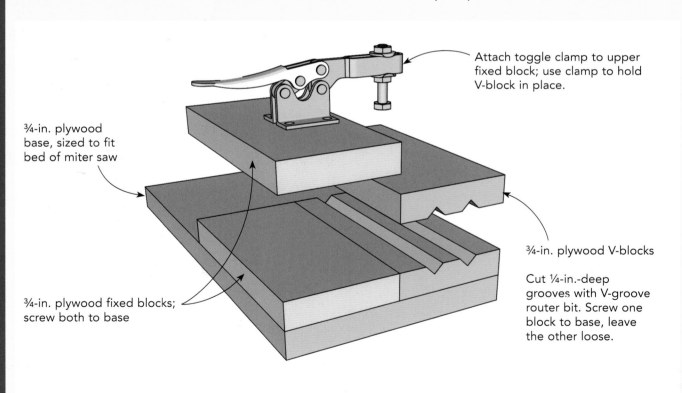

Attach toggle clamp to upper fixed block; use clamp to hold V-block in place.

¾-in. plywood base, sized to fit bed of miter saw

¾-in. plywood V-blocks

Cut ¼-in.-deep grooves with V-groove router bit. Screw one block to base, leave the other loose.

¾-in. plywood fixed blocks; screw both to base

Assemble the Seat Frame

Use a strong hardwood, such as ash or oak, to construct the seat frame. I prefer to use floating tenons to hold the frame together, but you can use conventional mortise-and-tenon joinery instead.

Mill pieces 3 in. wide and ¾ in. thick. Measure lengths directly from the chair. Make the front-to-back rails the distance between the front and back stretchers, minus ¼ in. Make the side-to-side rails the distance between the legs, minus ¼ in. Add at least 1½ in. to the side-to-side rails to allow for tenons, if necessary.

Chop away a small triangle of wood at each corner, to remove any sharp edges that could poke through the upholstery. Finally, chamfer or round over the top edges of the frame, again to protect the padding and upholstery. Take the frame to an upholstery shop, to have them make the seat and back cushions.

SIMPLE SEAT FRAME. Make the frame for the seat cushion from pieces of secondary wood, held with mortise-and-tenon joints.

UNSHARPEN EDGES. To protect the padding and upholstery, chamfer the corners and top edges of the seat frame.

TIME TO RELAX. Plop the cushions in place, then have a seat and take things easy.

Seat Frame and Cushions

Cushions are not included in the plans, and I recommend that you have them made by a professional upholsterer.

The seat cushion measures 6 in. thick by 23 in. wide by 25 in. long; it is built on a hardwood frame with 3-in. webbing stretched across the opening in the frame. The padding consists of 5 in. of high-density urethane foam wrapped in 1 in. of batting, covered with fabric or leather.

The back cushion measures 5 in. thick by 21 in. wide by 24 in. long. The padding in this case is 3 in. of high-density urethane foam wrapped in 1 in. of batting, covered with matching fabric or leather.

Seat Frame

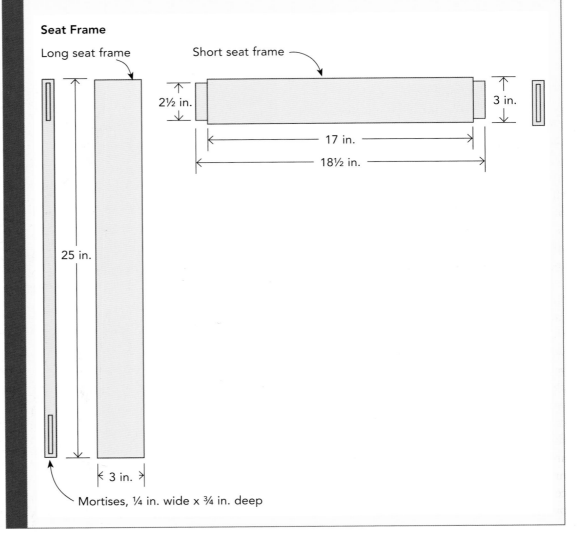

Long seat frame

Short seat frame

2½ in.

3 in.

17 in.

18½ in.

25 in.

3 in.

Mortises, ¼ in. wide x ¾ in. deep

GOOD OPTIONS FOR FINISHING

Countless books have been written about finishing, so one chapter in this book can't teach you all you need to know about the subject. However, I will provide some straightforward techniques tailored to the Arts & Crafts projects in this book. I'll share a simple finishing method that will leave a silky-smooth finish on any type of wood. Then I'll show how to color your Arts & Crafts project using traditional or modern methods, so your contemporary creation can fit in next to an antique original.

Finishing is a two- or three-stage process. The first stage for every project is thorough surface preparation. It is the foundation for all the work that follows. The other two stages enhance the wood's beauty and protect its surface. Typically, you color the wood with dyes, stains, or other chemicals. If you like the natural look of the wood, you can skip the coloring. Then you apply one of several protective coatings. The variety of finishes available today can be overwhelming, and most of the products on the market are significantly more durable than the ones applied a century ago. But remember, those "inferior" products have endured.

Surface Prep Is Critical

A fantastic finish begins with surface preparation. It doesn't matter what comes later. If you don't properly prepare the foundation for the finish, the subsequent coats will never look good.

I do most of my surface prep with a random-orbit sander, one of the easiest, most efficient tools for the job. The sander spins the abrasive while wiggling it back and forth, in order to make sanding marks less conspicuous. I begin with 100-grit paper, which is coarse enough to remove the milling marks left by the jointer, planer, and tablesaw. However, if your piece has very noticeable machine marks, you may need to start with 80 or 60 grit.

Turn the sander on and let the weight of the tool do the work. Don't press down or exert any force on the sander. That will interfere with the random action and leave bad sanding swirls. Move the sander along the surface at about 1 in. per second. Overlap your passes on wider boards and panels. If you use a vacuum to collect dust, put it on the lowest suction setting; or, if it has just one speed, use it to pick up dust between grits. A strong vacuum will pull the sander against the workpiece, cancelling the random-orbit action. When sanding endgrain, use a light touch to avoid introducing cross-grain scratches onto the surface.

EFFICIENT SANDING. A random orbit sander creates an inconspicuous scratch pattern. Here, on Plexiglas®, the pattern shows clearly. On wood, the sanding makes surfaces look and feel smooth.

WORK SMART

Sanding narrow edges and curves is most easily done by hand. I use a sanding block on long narrow edges and convex curves. For concave edges, such as the arch on the bottom of the bookcase (p. 40), I create a sanding strip and attach adhesive-backed sandpaper to that. The sanding strip helps distribute pressure, so I don't accidentally create a divot or hollow.

Once all the machine marks are gone, sand the piece again with increasingly finer grits. I switch to 120 and then 150 grit if I'm working with a coarse or open-grain wood such as oak, mahogany, or walnut. If I'm working with a fine-grain wood, like maple or cherry, I'll continue up to 180 grit.

Before each new round of sanding, clean the surfaces with compressed air or a vacuum. Pieces of the coarser abrasive undoubtedly wore off the paper and lodged in the workpiece. You don't want any of that coarser grit getting caught in the finer paper and making new sanding swirls.

OBVIOUS FLAW. Clean surfaces well between sanding grits, using a vacuum or compressed air. Otherwise, bits of abrasive left from previous grits can scar an otherwise flawless surface.

CAREFUL AT THE CORNERS. To reduce cross-grain scratches, avoid contacting adjacent surfaces when easing the edges, especially at the end of a board.

SOME EDGES STAY SHARP. Don't ease the edges on boards that come together, as shown here. Doing so will create a shadow line, making the joint seem sloppy.

When you have finished all the flat sanding, go over the sharp edges and corners. You don't want to leave any edge or corner so sharp that it's unpleasant to touch. Some folks just "break" the sharp edges with a few strokes of sandpaper, while others round over all the edges. To break the edges, fold a piece of 150- or 180-grit paper and sand by hand, holding the paper at an angle, until the sharp edge is gone. It only takes a few seconds.

Avoid easing edges or sanding the surfaces that will be concealed. For example, no one will ever see the top edges of the upper cross rails on the tabouret in chapter 3. There's no need to spend time sanding them. If you ease the top edges of those rails, you'll introduce a shadow line between the rail and the top, creating what appears to be a poorly fitting piece.

A Natural Finish as Simple as 3, 2, 1

One of the simplest finishes to apply is a wiping varnish known as 321. It provides a fair amount of protection and imparts a nice amber glow to most woods. It gives white oak a beautiful golden appearance and transforms cherry from salmon pink to a rich, deep reddish-brown. A wiping varnish can be used by itself, or you can

use it to protect wood you've dyed or stained; the colorings don't offer any protection on their own. Although you can buy ready-made wiping varnishes, I prefer to make my own from three parts turpentine or mineral spirits, two parts oil-based polyurethane, and one part boiled linseed oil. Those proportions explain the name of the finish. The definitive source of 321 is unknown, but many experts credit its popularity to woodworking legend Tage Frid, during his time teaching at Rochester Institute of Technology.

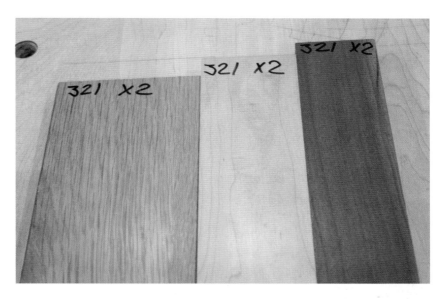

VERSATILE FINISH. My 321 finish works well on any type of wood, regardless of its grain structure or porosity. Shown here, from left to right, two coats of the finish applied to oak, maple, and cherry.

INGREDIENTS. The 321 finish consists of mineral spirits, polyurethane, and boiled linseed oil. When buying polyurethane, read the label carefully. The can on the right is water-based and will not be compatible with the finish.

READ CAREFULLY. Pure tung oil and tung oil finish are not the same thing. Tung oil finishes are thinned, and are essentially commercial versions of 321. Do not use them to create your own 321 finish.

KEEP IT TOGETHER. The ingredients in a 321 finish can separate easily because of their different densities. Here, one ingredient has formed that dark layer at the bottom of the jar. Stir the finish regularly during use.

SANDING AND FILLING. As you wet-sand, sawdust combines with finish to create a slurry that fills the grain of the wood. Here, I've made a squiggle through the slurry with my finger.

You can buy the ingredients for 321 at any hardware store or home center. I mix my batches in a Mason jar, which has graduations on the side. Begin with three parts mineral spirits. If you find the odor of mineral spirits objectionable, use odorless turpentine instead. Add two parts oil-based polyurethane. I use poly with a satin sheen. Avoid "oil modified" and waterborne polyurethanes; they aren't compatible with 321. The last ingredient is one part boiled linseed oil. You can substitute pure tung oil, although it's twice the price of boiled linseed oil and much harder to find. Stir the mixture thoroughly, and stir it regularly in use to keep the ingredients mixed.

Flood the finish onto the workpiece. Don't worry about grain direction, even coverage, appearance, or anything else. I use disposable foam brushes for this part of the job. Next, hand-sand the wet finish into the wood using 400-grit wet-or-dry paper. This creates a slurry that is suspended in the finish and helps smooth the surface by filling the wood grain.

Once you have done the sanding, remove the excess with a clean rag, rubbing as if you were trying to get stubborn dirt off the surface. Let

Damp or wet rags used with solvents and oil finishes, such as 321, pose a fire hazard. Spread them out on a nonflammable surface and allow them to dry thoroughly before disposal.

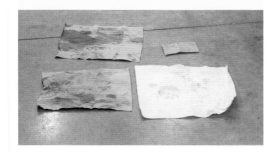

FUEL FOR FUMING. Janitorial-strength ammonia, left, can be used to fume wood but needs time to work. Industrial-strength ammonia, right, works quickly but is very hazardous. Regular household ammonia is too weak for fuming.

this initial coat dry completely. That may take a day or so, depending on the temperature and humidity. Don't apply the second coat until the first is not sticky at all.

Apply the second coat just like the first, but put very little pressure on the sandpaper. This time, you just want to give the piece a light scuff-sanding to remove any dust that may have settled on the piece when drying. Again, thoroughly rub off all the liquid finish. Additional coats of 321 can dry in as little as three or four hours, but it may take a day or two for the oil finish to set in cooler or damper areas.

It takes two to three coats for the look and feel of 321 to develop. However, 321 is a thin finish, so I put a minimum of four coats on all surfaces. You may want to apply even more coats on surfaces that will see heavy wear such as tabletops or chair arms.

How to Create an Authentic Fumed Finish

One of the best known Arts & Crafts wood treatments is the fumed finish. Fuming takes its name from the exposure of the wood to ammo-

nia fumes, which react with the tannins in certain woods and cause a color change. Some brownish and reddish woods, including oak, cherry, and walnut, have a higher amount of tannins than woods like maple or pine. It has been said that farmers discovered fuming when they noticed the oak beams in their barns had turned a warm brown, particularly near horse stalls, where concentrations of ammonia were higher. The story may be apocryphal, but it is plausible. The science behind fuming, on the other hand, is undeniable.

You can't use just any old ammonia to fume wood. Household ammonia from the supermarket won't work because it's too weak. You have to use janitorial-strength or industrial-strength ammonia. Of the two, janitorial strength is less hazardous and easier to obtain. You can get it at most hardware stores. For the industrial-strength stuff, you'll need to go to a chemical supply source.

Industrial-strength ammonia will cause skin burns, respiratory complications, and can send you to the emergency room. You must wear a good quality organic vapor respirator, heavy-duty gloves, heavy clothing, and full-coverage eye

QUICK COVER. A fuming tent is simple and straightforward to build. It's made from scraps that are screwed together and covered with plastic (here, I'm using heavy-duty garbage bags).

Industrial-strength ammonia fumes can be lethal. Wear a respirator, goggles, and heavy-duty gloves, as shown here.

protection. Read the material safety data sheet (MSDS) that applies to the ammonia you obtain, and follow the manufacturer's safety recommendations. Work outdoors with industrial-strength ammonia.

By contrast, you won't need lots of protective gear with janitorial-strength ammonia (unless you have a sensitivity to the chemical), and you can use it indoors. Because it's weaker than industrial-strength ammonia, janitorial ammonia takes longer to work.

In order to fume wood, you need something to concentrate the fumes. In old days, woodworkers used tar-impregnated canvas tarps to cover the workpiece and keep the ammonia fumes from dissipating. Today, plastic sheeting works just fine. I generally build a simple framework from scrap wood and attach plastic to it to make a small tent for fuming. You can simply drape plastic over your project, too.

Despite the potential hazards, fuming is very simple. Pour some ammonia into a glass or heavy plastic dish and put it under the workpiece. Cover the piece with the tent or plastic sheeting. Now walk away—that's all there is to it.

The quantity of tannins in the wood, the ambient temperature, and the amount of time the wood is exposed to the fumes impact the final color of the piece. When I fume, I keep the wood exposed for about 36 hours, when the daytime temperature is about 70 degrees. This turns the wood a deep brown, with grayish-green undertones. You'll want to experiment with the duration of the fuming to get the color you desire. Put a piece of scrap wood under the plastic sheeting and check it periodically to see how the color changes. And keep in mind that tannin concentration is out of your control, so the results from fuming will not be completely predictable.

When the piece has fumed long enough for your satisfaction, remove the plastic and let it air out a bit. Pour any remaining ammonia back into its original container and wash the dish immediately with soap and water. You can use

BEFORE AND AFTER. The left half of this piece of oak has been fumed, which leaves the surface slightly darkened and dull. Applying a finish, however, makes the grain and figure really pop.

the ammonia over and over until it has completely evaporated.

Once the fumes have dissipated, apply a top-coat of oil, wiping varnish like my 321, or shellac to bring out the wood's true beauty. If the fumed wood looks a little dull, you can also apply a stain before the clear finish.

The Basics of Stains and Dyes

Like fuming, stains and dyes color the wood. But unlike fuming, stains produce very predictable results and are much safer. I prefer an oil-based stain, which I brush on to the wood, let set for a short period of time, and then wipe off the excess.

Stains contain pigment (finely ground colored granules, such as red clay or lampblack) suspended in a solvent (mineral spirits, for example) and combined with a binder such as linseed oil that helps the pigment stick to the wood. The pigment granules get caught in the sanding marks and the wood grain. So oak and other woods with big, open grain tend to stain darker and have more contrast than woods with tight, closed grain, such as maple or cherry.

Some of the stains I have used for Arts & Crafts projects have names like Early American,

BIG DIFFERENCE. The maple (left) and oak are stained with the same pecan oil stain. The open grain of the oak holds more pigment, so it goes darker than the tight-grained maple.

GO-TO STAINS. These are a few of the colors I use regularly on Arts & Crafts furniture projects. From left to right, they are Dark Walnut, Red Mahogany, and Early American.

Dark Walnut, and Red Mahogany. You'll want to experiment with different colors and different brands to get the look you're after. (Stain colors or names aren't uniform from brand to brand.) Keep in mind that the topcoat you apply will affect the final color.

Most of the authentic Stickley and Roycroft furniture I come across is a warm reddish-brown, with very prominent ray flake. To duplicate that look, you could fume the piece and

DYE AND STAIN. Before staining this board, I applied a reddish dye, which you can see at the left. The two finishes work well together to accentuate the grain and figure.

DISTINCTIVE APPEARANCE. For the most part, quartersawn white oak has an open, porous grain. The ray flake stands out because its grain is very fine, more like that of maple or cherry.

wait a century, but it's faster to use a combination of dyes and stains, which will make the ray flake in quartersawn white oak really pop.

Dyes consist of pigment and solvent, and the particles of dye pigment are much, much smaller than those in oil stains. (I prefer water-based dyes, but you can use an alcohol-based dye instead. However, I'd avoid oil-based dyes, which will react with oil stain and produce a muddy color.)

Opaque Finishes

Paint or tinted lacquer were not that common to Arts & Crafts pieces. Because part of the Arts & Crafts philosophy was to use the wood itself to beautify the project, most furniture makers shied away from opaque finishes. However, a few makers and designers, most notably Charles Rennie Mackintosh, embraced opaque finishes. They often used stark, solid black and white to emphasize both contrast and harmony in the environments they designed.

A dye binds to the wood more consistently than an oil stain, which tends to collect in sanding scratches and areas of open grain, but not in denser areas. The grain of quartersawn oak is very porous, while the ray flake is very dense. So you can color the wood very uniformly with dye, then color the porous parts with an oil stain. The two-stage coloring really makes the ray flake stand out.

Dyes are great when used on their own, but you need to keep basic color theory in mind when using a dye with a stain. As we learned early on in life, two colors mixed together can yield a distinctly different result: yellow and blue make green, green and red make brown, and so on. I use an antique cherry water-based aniline dye, mixing 1 oz. of powder in 1 qt. of water. Follow the dye manufacturer's mixing instructions. Practice on scraps before you begin coloring the workpiece, to be sure the dye is strong enough and works well with the stain color.

Apply the dye with a disposable foam brush, following with a rag to wipe off the excess immediately. Dyes color wood the instant they

DYED OAK. Dyes color wood consistently and uniformly, regardless of the grain structure or porosity.

DON'T OVERDO THE SANDING. Scuff-sanding can produce a slight color variation, shown on the left side of the board. That's normal. Areas sanded through (right side of board), obviously need to be touched up with more dye.

make contact. They don't need to sit on the wood like an oil-based stain does. Maintain a wet edge while applying the dye to avoid streaks. Allow the project to dry overnight. The dye will raise the wood grain, so scuff-sand the piece with 220-grit paper. You want to remove nibs of grain. Touch up severe sand-throughs with more dye, followed by another overnight drying and scuff-sanding.

Once the dye has dried completely, apply the oil-based stain. Shake the stain vigorously to distribute the pigment, then brush it on quickly. Stir the stain regularly to keep the heavy pigment suspended. Once you've stained the entire piece, wipe off the excess. With larger pieces, or if the stain seems to dry too quickly, work on half the project at a time.

After about an hour, wipe down the piece again. Some oil-based stains have a tendency to bleed from the large pores of the oak. When the stain is completely dry, apply a protective topcoat, such as 321.

WIPE AND WIPE. I use two rags at a time to wipe off finish. The one in my left hand removes excess liquid, while the one in my right hand absorbs the residue. As the left-hand rag becomes saturated, I replace it with the rag from my right hand and get a clean rag for that hand.

Sources of Supply for Arts & Crafts Hardware

A somewhat selective listing of companies that offer knobs, pulls, hinges, latches, and other fittings.

ACORN MANUFACTURING
457 School St.
Mansfield, MA 02048
800-835-0121
acornmfg.com

ATG STORES
11730 118th Ave. N.E., #100
Kirkland, WA 98034
888-500-9541
atgstores.com

BALDWIN HARDWARE
1 Meridian Blvd., Ste. 1A02
Wyomissing, PA 19610
800-566-1986
baldwinhardware.com

BAUERWARE CABINET HARDWARE
3886 17th St.
San Francisco, CA 94114
415-864-5662
bauerware.com

CHARLESTON HARDWARE COMPANY
2143 A Heriot St.
Charleston, SC 29403
866-958-8626
charlestonhardwareco.com

CIRECAST
1790 Yosemite Ave.
San Francisco, CA 94124
415-822-3030
cirecast.com

CRAFTSMAN HARDWARE
370 N.E. Camano Dr., Ste. 5-137
Camano Island, WA 98282
509-766-4322
craftsmanhardware.com

CRAFTSMAN HOMES CONNECTION
2525 E. 29th, Ste. 10B-343
Spokane, WA 99223
509-535-5098
crafthome.com

CRAFTSMEN HARDWARE
P.O. Box 161
Marceline, MO 64658
660-376-2481
craftsmenhardware.com

CROWN CITY HARDWARE
1047 N. Allen Ave.
Pasadena, CA 91104
626-794-0234
restoration.com

EUGENIA'S ANTIQUE HARDWARE AND ACCESSORIES
5370 Peachtree Rd.
Chamblee, GA 30341
770-458-1677
eugeniaantiquehardware.com

HAMILTON SINKLER
31 E. 32nd St., Fl. 11
New York, NY 10016
212-760-3377
hamiltonsinkler.com

HISTORIC HOUSEPARTS
528–540 South Ave.
Rochester, NY 14620
888-558-2329
historichouseparts.com

HORTON BRASSES
49 Nooks Hill Rd.
Cromwell, CT 06416
800-754-9127
horton-brasses.com

HOUSE OF ANTIQUE HARDWARE
802 N.E. Davis St.
Portland, OR 97232
888-223-2545
houseofantiquehardware.com

LB BRASS

7021 Sterling Ponds Ct.

Sterling Heights, MI 48312

888-644-1570

lbbrass.com

LEE VALLEY & VERITAS

P.O. Box 1780

Ogdensburg, NY 13669-6780

800-871-8158

leevalley.com/US/Hardware

LIZ'S ANTIQUE HARDWARE

453 S. La Brea Ave.

Los Angeles, CA 90036

323-939-4403

lahardware.com

NOTTING HILL DECORATIVE HARDWARE

P.O. Box 1376

Lake Geneva, WI 53147

262-248-8890

nottinghill-usa.com

OAK PARK HOME & HARDWARE

137 N. Oak Park Ave., Ste. 115

Oak Park, IL 60301

773-836-3606

oakparkhome-hardware.com

OLD HOUSE PARTS CO.

1 Trackside Dr.

Kennebunk, ME 04043

207-985-1999

oldhouseparts.com

REJUVENATION

2550 NW Nicolai St.

Portland, OR 97210

888-401-1900

rejuvenation.com

ROCKY MOUNTAIN HARDWARE

P.O. Box 4108

1030 Airport Way

Hailey, ID 83333

888-788-2013

rockymountainhardware.com

SIGNATURE HARDWARE

2700 Crescent Springs Pike

Erlanger, KY 41017

866-855-2284

signaturehardware.com

SMITH WOODWORKS & DESIGN

427 County Rd. 513

Califon, NJ 07830

908-832-2723

niceknobs.com

SUN VALLEY BRONZE

P.O. Box 3475

Hailey, ID 83333

866-788-3631

svbronze.com

VAN DYKE'S RESTORERS

P.O. Box 52

Louisiana, MO 63353

800-558-1234

vandykes.com

VINTAGE HARDWARE & LIGHTING

2000 Sims Way

Port Townsend, WA 98368

360-379-9030

vintagehardware.com

Metric Equivalents

INCHES	CENTIMETERS	MILLIMETERS	INCHES	CENTIMETERS	MILLIMETERS
1/8	0.3	3	13	33.0	330
1/4	0.6	6	14	35.6	356
3/8	1.0	10	15	38.1	381
1/2	1.3	13	16	40.6	406
5/8	1.6	16	17	43.2	432
3/4	1.9	19	18	45.7	457
7/8	2.2	22	19	48.3	483
1	2.5	25	20	50.8	508
1 1/4	3.2	32	21	53.3	533
1 1/2	3.8	38	22	55.9	559
1 3/4	4.4	44	23	58.4	584
2	5.1	51	24	61	610
2 1/2	6.4	64	25	63.5	635
3	7.6	76	26	66.0	660
3 1/2	8.9	89	27	68.6	686
4	10.2	102	28	71.7	717
4 1/2	11.4	114	29	73.7	737
5	12.7	127	30	76.2	762
6	15.2	152	31	78.7	787
7	17.8	178	32	81.3	813
8	20.3	203	33	83.8	838
9	22.9	229	34	86.4	864
10	25.4	254	35	88.9	889
11	27.9	279	36	91.4	914
12	30.5	305			

If you like this book, you'll love *Fine Woodworking*.

Read *Fine Woodworking* Magazine:

Get seven issues, including our annual *Tools & Shops* issue, plus FREE tablet editions. Packed with trusted expertise, every issue helps build your skills as you build beautiful, enduring projects.

Subscribe today at:
FineWoodworking.com/4Sub

Shop our *Fine Woodworking* Online Store:

It's your destination for premium resources from America's best craftsmen: how-to books, DVDs, project plans, special interest publications, and more.

Visit today at:
FineWoodworking.com/4More

Get our FREE *Fine Woodworking* eNewsletter:

Improve your skills, find new project ideas, and enjoy free tips and advice from *Fine Woodworking* editors.

Sign up, it's free:
FineWoodworking.com/4Newsletter

Become a FineWoodworking.com Member

Join to enjoy unlimited access to premium content and exclusive benefits, including: 1,400 in-depth articles, over 400 videos from top experts, tablet editions, contests, special offers, and more.

Find more information online:
FineWoodworking.com/4Join

The Taunton Press

© 2014 The Taunton Press